HELEN R. TROBIAN

1368

THE INSTRUMENTAL ENSEMBLE IN THE CHURCH

THE INSTRUMENTAL ENSEMBLE IN THE CHURCH

Portions of this book first appeared as articles in *Music Ministry*, and are used by permission.

SET UP, PRINTED, AND BOUND BY THE PARTHENON PRESS, AT NASHVILLE, TENNESSEE, UNITED STATES OF AMERICA

PREFACE

It is hoped that this book will help to establish the importance of instrumental music in the church. There are many ways in which instrumental ensembles can contribute to the expression of worship, to the fellowship and service functions of the church, to the program of religious education, and to the church's outreach into the community. This book presents a general outlook toward the use of instrumental music in churches and some resources for those who wish to use ensemble music appropriately.

Paul in his letter to the Galatians described the fruit of the Spirit as "love, joy, peace, patience, kindness, goodness, faithfulness, gentleness, self-control" (5:22). Instrumental ensembles are media that can nurture these fruits both for the participating musicians and for congregational listeners.

To the Rev. V. Earle Copes the writer wishes to express appreciation for suggesting this book. Not the least of the contributions to this endeavor has been the consonant interests of my husband Albert Trobian.

HELEN R. TROBIAN

CONTENTS

CONTENTS

CHAPTER I

Ensembles in Worship

The use of instrumental-ensemble music in American churches is gradually increasing. In the past many of those who planned and directed church music were organists or vocalists unacquainted with instruments and the instrumental repertory. Today's professional church musician is broadly trained and capable of rendering a variety of musical services in addition to choir training and organ playing. In the past instrumental performers were not always available. Now that the public school music program includes bands and orchestras and pupils have the opportunity to learn to play an instrument as part of the curriculum, many students and graduates are capable of church performance. Also there are more conservatory graduates and professional musicians available.

The history of music shows clearly and dramatically that musicians of merit have been seriously interested in composing instrumental as well as vocal music for use in church services. Instrumental music is of especial value for expressing those ideas which cannot be verbalized. In this type of music ideas are expressed in generalized and relative aspects. Instrumental music does not have to tell a story or paint a picture. Words have many associations and connotations, but an instrumental composition that has been symbolically inspired may convey to those who hear it a purifying spiritual message.

Since music of an appropriate character tends to intensify religious consciousness, it functions best when it is appropriate to the particular stage of the worship process. Worship arises from and is satisfying to certain universal human needs. Some of these are the need for peace and inner harmony, for forgiveness, and for moral leadership.

Within a specific service human needs find satisfaction through various acts of worship. The general structure of the service usually progresses through adoration, confession, petition, illumination or challenge, dedication or rapport. Therefore, to satisfy the needs of individual worshipers and to contribute most to the systematic structure of the service, music must be well planned. There is much instrumental music for ensembles that expresses praise and adoration. There is also much that emphasizes quiet dignity or that produces a mood conducive to problem solving. Reverent music bordering on the mysterious can help in setting up a receptive attitude. For the strength and courage necessary to dedication and rededication there is music combining tender, ardent devotion with solemnity and grandeur.

In the church of today instrumental ensembles playing appropriate music may contribute to the importance of the service, unify the congregation, and enrich the religious experience of the group. Many types of ensembles can be effective. One or more brass, woodwind, or string instruments with organ, trios and quartets, brass choirs, string orchestras, small orchestras—all may be used to enhance the worship experience.

Such musical offerings relieve the monotony of standardized procedure. Church members take more interest in regular attendance when the service has occasional variety. Good public relations for the church, both within the congregation and its administration and with others, will be fostered by attention to variations in the music program designed to retain interest and to stimulate religious experience. One can greatly enrich the worship services of a church by developing instrumental ensembles composed of capable players from the congregation.

For the purpose of listing examples of instrumental ensemble music for use in worship services six categories expressing human feelings related to worship have been chosen:

1. Praise and adoration
2. Penitence and somber feeling
3. Conflict ending in triumph
4. Tranquility, peace, and contentment
5. Hope and aspiration
6. Cheerfulness and joy

This list is only suggestive and is intended to indicate the type of material that might be used with various kinds of ensembles to meet the need for instrumental music in worship services. All the items are available through most music stores. One should

9

indicate composer, title, and publisher when ordering. The final letter after each, indicates the degree of difficulty: E, easy; M, moderately difficult; D, difficult.

1. **Praise and Adoration**
   Piano with Brass Quartet:

Favorite Festival Carols	Volkwein	E

   Organ with Brass Quartet:

Glazunov	Rubank	E
In Modo Religioso		
Ravenello	J. Fischer	M
Christus Resurrexit		

   Orchestra:

Brahms	Broude	M
O God Thou Holiest		
Palestrina	Galaxy	M
Adoramus Te and Sanctus		

   String Orchestra:

Bach	Volkwein	M
Mystical Adoration		

   Brass Septet:

Di Lasso	Robert King	M
Providebaum Dominum		

   Four Trombones:

Haubiel	Henri Elkan	M
Recessional		

   Flute, Oboe, Horn, Clarinet, Bassoon:

Bach-Hirsh	C. Fischer	M-D
Fugue in E Flat		

   Flute, Clarinet, Bassoon:

Bach-Tarlow	Galaxy	M-D
Fugue in C Minor		

   Flute, Oboe, Clarinet, Horn, Bassoon, or Four Clarinets:

Bach	Rubank	E
The Light of All Our Seeing		

2. **Penitence and Somber Feeling**
   Orchestra:

Bach	Broude	D

10

Adagio from Brandenburg
Concerto No. 1 in F
Brass Choir:
   Purcell   Robert King   M
     Music for the Funeral of Queen Mary
Three Trombones, One Trumpet:
   Beethoven-Kahn   Edward B.   M-D
     Equali for Four Trombones   Marks

3. Conflict Ending in Triumph

String Quartet:
   Beethoven   Peters   D
     Quartet No. 15 in A Minor
      (3rd or 3rd, 4th, and last
      movements)
   Beethoven   Peters   D
     Quartet No. 12 in E Flat Major
Brass Choir:
   Gabrieli-Harvey   Galaxy   M-D
     Sonata Pian e Forte

4. Tranquility, Peace, and Contentment

Orchestra:
   Handel-Holst   Volkwein   M-D
     Pastoral Symphony from Messiah
Strings, Flute, Clarinet:
   Bach-Gaul   Volkwein   M
     Sheep May Safely Graze
Three Clarinets:
   Beethoven   Cundy-Bettoney   M
     Adagio Cantabile from Trio, Op. 87
Brass Quartet:
   Bortniansky   Rubank   E
     Divine Praise

5. Hope and Aspiration

Organ, Violin, Harp:
   Dickinson, C.   H. W. Gray   M

11

Exaltation

Small Orchestra:

Handel	Rubank	M
Largo from Xerxes		
Bach	Oxford	M
Sleepers, Wake		

String Orchestra:

Bach	Galaxy	M
Come, Sweet Death		

String Quartet and Clarinet:

Mozart	Cundy-Bettoney
Larghetto from Quintet in A for Clarinet and Strings, K. 581	

Clarinet Quartet:

Mozart	Rubank	E
Ave Verum Corpus		

Brass Quartet:

Mendelssohn	Cundy-Bettoney	E
I Waited for the Lord from Hymn of Praise		
Verdi	Rubank	E
There Shall Be Singing		

6. Cheerfulness and Joy

Orchestra:

Mendelssohn	C. Fischer	M
Overture to A Midsummer Night's Dream		

Violin, Viola, Cello:

Gibbons	Theodore Presser	M
Four Fantasies for Strings		
Purcell	Theodore Presser	M
Three Fantasies		

Two Trumpets, Two Trombones:

Schein	Theodore Presser	M
Intrada and Paduana		
Bach	Rubank	E
Triumphant Rose the Son of God		

12

CHAPTER II

Ensembles in Christian Education

Personal and social integration of individuals is an aim of the Christian education program. This aim is approached through the beneficial results which accrue from the satisfaction of physical, emotional, social, and educational needs. As one of the activities of the Christian-education program, the instrumental ensemble has the capacity to satisfy these needs simultaneously.

The playing of string, wind, and percussion instruments provides satisfying tactile sensations and beneficial rhythmic experiences. Here is a physical activity on an aesthetic level which allows the unified participation of a wide range of ages and abilities, a strengthening factor to the church as a whole.

Music is essentially a social art. In the instrumental ensemble there is opportunity for one to develop consideration for and co-operation with others and to learn to subordinate his own individuality to the good of the group. "You shall love your neighbor as yourself" operates as a socializing principle. Each participant must de-emphasize his own egocentricity in order that his interpretation of the music may match that achieved by the whole group.

Playing an instrument in a group affords an excellent opportunity for emotional expression and fulfills a need for closer human relationships. The success of the

13

group depends on the social and musical congeniality of its members.

In an ensemble each person has a dual function as leader and as follower. At times he must dominate the expression of the group, while at other times he must follow or accompany other members. The type of self-control called for on the part of the members of a music ensemble develops patience and encourages poise and courtesy. The individual member of the group learns to take criticism, to be accurate and to desire accuracy, and to recognize the importance of attention to details.

The instrumental music ensemble lends itself admirably for use in Christian education because it does not focus on individual recognition or rewards. Here is a medium which can easily serve as a center around which other interests could be formed—a medium usable for many occasions in church life. By its essential nature it lends itself to developing the ideal of service for others.

Ensemble playing is an immediately meaningful experience. Here it is possible to know the joyous experience of preoccupation with unselfish interests and the elevation of feeling that comes from contact with the beautiful in music. Much of the music which has lived through the centuries has come to us from the hands of inspired, devout composers. When we play it after studying it sincerely we participate to some degree in their aesthetic creativity.

Many adults who played instruments when they

14

were in school or college have not touched them for years. Frequently the reason is not lack of desire, but lack of a group in which to play. For such persons the establishment of small groups to play various types of music fills a real need. These groups could begin by playing easy music. Good music is not necessarily difficult. They need feel no necessity for public performance. If desired the ensembles can be formed with the sole aim of playing together.

One trend today in church youth programs is toward fellowship. This indicates a conscious effort on the part of young people to maintain their organizations in a democratic fashion, endeavoring to recognize the needs of all persons and making an effort to meet those needs. Major needs of youth, such as social participation, acceptance, freedom, and opportunity to express emotions, are well met by youth fellowships.

The instrumental ensemble contributes specifically to these needs. Ensembles provide a splendid opportunity for young people to learn habits and skills which are desirable to social living and to future vocational adjustment. Not only the spirit of co-operation, but also reliability and initiative of each individual are developed. There is also the opportunity, which is sometimes neglected, for purposeful evaluation. Wise leaders will allow the youth to evaluate their own skills and abilities, thereby adding to the development of their aesthetic judgment and growth in their appreciation of art forms.

In organizing ensembles for children who are be-

15

ginners on their instruments, care must be taken to provide playable music for all participants. It is a satisfying experience for the child to play a simple hymn tune that is well within his ability. All parts should be in appropriate playing range, be an actual part of the harmonic structure, and have rhythmic and melodic interest. Elementary players should have a hand in the management of their group. Whenever possible and advisable they may perform for others. In church-school groups there are various opportunities to correlate music and study. For example, during the study of the Old Testament rams' horns can be obtained and made into horns such as the shofar. While studying the Psalms of David, the children can make simple lyres or harps of string or wire and can compose simple songs.

Churches are sometimes hosts to conventions, rallies, or other meetings where ensemble music can contribute to the friendliness of the general atmosphere—especially during a period of registration or during interludes for getting acquainted. When ensembles are asked to play for meetings, the members may discuss the function they have in the total structure of the meeting and make certain they play music appropriate to the particular situation.

In some localities the women of the church help to raise the budget by a regular schedule of dinners for such groups as Rotary Club, Kiwanis Club, and Men's Forum, or by serving convention dinners. Some churches sponsor a weekly church night with a potluck

16

supper. For these events a small dinner orchestra can be a means of producing a group feeling of dignified informality. An orchestra playing pleasant music can bridge the period of time between the arrival of guests and the seating for dinner. The situation will determine whether the orchestra plays during dinner. If it does, it is best that it play softly and that it be some distance from the dinner tables. Members of the ensembles may take turns in management and leadership. If the group consists of less than five or six players, or if they are a mature group accustomed to playing together, they will probably perform without a conductor. More frequently a conductor will be necessary. Here is a splendid opportunity for student conductors, since dinner music should not be very difficult.

The recent emphasis on family-life education has caused churches to study needs of families and survey resources available to meet these needs. One of the finest ideas coming out of this study is the idea of the church sponsored "family night at home." A family ensemble can work together in a recreational capacity and can also help in creating a sense of aesthetic self-realization. It can enhance the value of group worship during periods of family worship. Modern life has a tendency to separate the family in their recreational activities. The playing of instruments is an excellent means of recreation, tending to unify the family's activities at home and at church and allowing the individual to take part rather than be a spectator, as he so often is in our society. Family activities within the

17

church provide excellent occasions for ensembles to play. At times a series of family groups may participate together to form a larger music unit.

The establishment of ensembles in the program of Christian education provides a link between the church and the school which will help to further good relationships in areas other than music.

If the program of Christian education is to reach out into the community and minister to the needs of the people that program should seek to help not only its members, but other members of the community as well. Ensembles can make a valuable socializing contribution by providing co-operative activity media for the church's relations with other institutions.

Frequently the various organizations of the church can use ensemble music advantageously in the interlocking areas of fellowship, service, and worship. Ensemble music can be used within the structure of the organization and in the extension of its efforts to the life of the church.

Instrumental trios will probably be the most easily organized ensembles in any of the existing organizations. Piano and any two instruments chosen from flute, oboe, clarinet, horn, bassoon, trumpet, trombone, violin, viola, or cello make an interesting trio.

There may be instances where an orchestra can be formed as an autonomous enterprise. This may be a point of contact for someone who has no interest in any other church organization. From interest in an orchestra other interests may be gradually elicited as the participant becomes more cognizant of the work of the church. An orchestra may translate its functions into terms of recreation and fellowship, missionary activity, aids to worship, or assistance in the work of another organization. It may serve as a stimulus for other arts groups in the church—the graphic arts, handcrafts, dramatics.

As a basis for organization of ensembles it will be advisable to keep in mind:

1. Instrumentation.
2. Ability of performers.
3. Age and compatibility of persons.
4. Family and neighborhood groupings.

The selection of music may be one of the greatest factors contributing to successful performance. If a music library fund is available selection can be based on music needs of groups playing for church occasions with functions of fellowship, service, and worship. An interested person might donate funds for this purpose.

The music selected should be well within the abilities of those who are to play it. It should be appropriate to the occasion whether it be dinner music or music for a worship service.

CHAPTER III

Small Ensembles: String and Wind

Sonata da Chiesa and *the Trio Sonata*

While looking over programs of organ recitals I found that organists frequently invited instrumentalists to assist them in presenting an afternoon or evening program. Of the selections played that included other instrumentalists the most consistently recurring title was "trio sonata." Some composers represented were Corelli, Buxtehude, Krebs, Loeilliet, Haydn, Telemann, and Arne.

Because of my interest in the use of orchestral instruments in churches I explored the background of trio sonatas to see why organists had chosen them for their recitals. They were well oriented in their choice of this literature, as the forerunner of the trio sonata was the *sonata da chiesa*, or church sonata. Even now, a contemporary writer occasionally uses the title *sonata da chiesa*.

The church sonata has an interesting history, developing from the early instrumental canzone. In baroque society sonatas were used for the court, the theater, and the church. The *sonata da chiesa* as distinguished from the *sonata da camera*, or chamber sonata, was not supposed to include dance movements, yet an actual dance title occasionally heads a movement in a church sonata. While there was much overlapping in both function and terminology the church sonata has a more serious nature; it has a rich polyphonic texture and is likely to call for organ as the keyboard instrument rather than harpsichord. Without dance rhythms, with noble, unsentimental melodies, this music has a forthrightness which inspires the aesthetic outlook.

In Italy some of these instrumental selections were designated for use in the various sequences of the Mass. Outside Italy several historians mention such music played in the church in connection with Vespers. Being essentially a serious work in contrapuntal style the *sonata da chiesa* is still well adapted to its original function of contributing to the church service.

The instruments most used in addition to keyboard were two melody instruments and a bass instrument. The violin, the flute, and the oboe were the chief melody instruments; the viola da gamba and the violoncello were the chief bass instruments. There was also some use of bassoon and trombone. As a substitute for organ or harpsichord, the lute, the guitar, or the harp was used. There is evidence also of orchestral or multiple performance using several instruments on one part.

Gradually the *sonata da chiesa* and the *sonata da camera* began to influence each other. Finally the distinction disappeared and the relatively modern term "trio sonata" came into being.

Many of the trio sonatas are typical *sonatas da*

chiesa with four movements in slow-fast, slow-fast sequence. They were called three part sonatas, the keyboard instrument being taken for granted.

Arcangelo Corelli (1653-1713) wrote thirty church sonatas. With the exception of occasional moderately difficult bowing for violinists, they are easy to perform. They serve to illustrate a midpoint in the history of this particular form. Those especially worthy of mention before him include Marini and Buonamente. Outstanding musicians contemporary with Corelli who were writing in comparable forms were Legrenzi, Vitali, Purcell, and Buxtehude. Those who followed after were Veracini, Vivaldi, Tartini, Bach, and Handel.

The slow movements of many of the sonatas by these composers have an atmosphere of beauty and reverence, and the fast movements are in keeping with the serious intention of contributing to the church service of that time.

Trio sonatas are particularly usable for church concerts. They are quite appropriate since many of them had their first performance as a contribution to the services of a church, and they are not technically difficult to play. The nature of the music is such that if two violins are not available any duo combination chosen from flutes, oboes, or clarinets may substitute for melody instruments; a bassoon may substitute for cello, or where it duplicates the keyboard part it may be omitted if a modern organ or piano is being used. Some trio sonatas may be played as string or woodwind trios, omitting the keyboard part when using an adequate bass instrument.

The following is a selected list from the numerous possibilities. Except where instruments are listed all the sonatas are written for two violins and keyboard with optional violoncello.

Trio Sonatas for Church Usage

Abaco, dall'	Trio Sonata, Op. 3, No. 2 (2 flutes or violins)	Peters
Albinoni	Sonata da Chiesa á 3 in G Minor, Op. 8, No. 4a	E. C. Schirmer
Arne, T.	Trio Sonata in A, Op. 3, No. 1	Associated Music Publishers
Bach (Seiffert)	Trio from Musical Offering (violin, flute, keyboard [violoncello])	Associated Music Publishers
Bononcini, G.	Sonata á 3 in D Minor, Op. 1, No. 6	Associated Music Publishers
Corelli	Two Sonatas da Chiesa á 3, Op. 1 (No. 7 in C, No. 12 in D)	Associated Music Publishers
———	Sonatas da Chiesa, Op. 1, No. 10 in G Minor and Opus 3, No. 5 in D Minor	Associated Music Publishers
Fux	Sinfonia in F (flute, oboe, keyboard [violoncello])	Associated Music Publishers
———	Sonata Pastorale á 3 in F	Associated Music Publishers
Handel	Opus 2 (no violoncello), No. 3 in F; No. 4 in B Flat, No. 6, No. 7, and No. 8 each in G Minor; No. 9 in E	Peters

23

Handel (Seiffert)	No. 2 in D Minor, No. 4 in F, No. 6 in D (two oboes, bassoon or violoncello, and keyboard)	Associated Music Publishers
Haydn (Bergmann)	Trio in F, Op. 11, No. 4 (flute, violin, keyboard [violoncello])	Associated Music Publishers
Heinichen (Hausswald)	Sonata in G (flute, violin, keyboard [violoncello])	Associated Music Publishers
Krebs, J. (Riemann)	Trio in D (Flute or violin, violin, keyboard [violoncello])	Associated Music Publishers
Ruggieri, G. M. (Nowak)	Sonatas da Chiesa, Op. 3, No. 1 in E Minor, No. 2 in B Minor, No. 3 in B Flat, No. 4 in F, No. 5 in G Minor, No. 6 in A, No. 7 in A Minor, No. 8 in G, No. 9 in G Minor, No. 10 in D	Associated Music Publishers
Tartini	Sonata á 3 in D, Op. 8, No. 6	Associated Music Publishers
Uccellini	Sinfonia á 3 in A, Op. 9, No. 7	Associated Music Publishers
Vitali	Sonata á 3 in D Minor, Op. 2, No. 6	Associated Music Publishers
Vivaldi	Sonata á 3 in G Minor	Associated Music Publishers

String Quartets

The string quartet has been a profound medium for the expression of many types of feeling. The classic masters frequently used this form to demonstrate filial gratitude to their creator. Many slow movements of works for string quartet are described by musicologists as being in the nature of a prayer. Certain movements are described by critics as "noble" or "sublime."

One of the earliest known works for string quartet was composed by Giovanni Bononcini (ca. 1672-1752), a violoncellist at the church of San Petronio in Bologna. His *Sinfonie da Chiesa* for two violins, viola, and violoncello was written for performance in his church in 1687.

Maurizio Cazzati (ca. 1620-77), who was director of the San Petronio Chapel Orchestra, also published some string quartets in his *Sonata a due, tré, quattro, e cinque, con alcue per tromba, Op. 35* (1665). These very early string quartets were written for and played in the church.

Most Protestant hymnals contain at least one hymn set to the tune of "Pleyel's hymn." Ignaz Pleyel (1757-1831), a contemporary of Mozart, wrote the hymn as part of a string quartet. His *Quartet No. 4* consists of variations on this hymn. The adagio of his *Quartet, Op. 8, No. 1*, also shows religious feeling.

The second movement, *Larghetto sans lenteur*, of Cherubini's *First Quartet in E Flat* is in polyphonic devotional style. Another prayerlike larghetto is the *Larghetto in B Major* of César Franck's *D Major Quartet*. Wilhelm Altmann described it as a "splendid monument of purity, grandeur and artistic simplicity." Vincent d'Indy considered the adagio (second movement) of Beethoven's *Twelfth Quartet in E Flat, Op. 127*, to be the "most sublime" of prayers. In the *Fifteenth Quartet, Op. 132 in A Minor* by Beethoven

25

(1770-1827) the third movement carries the superscription "Holy Song of Thanksgiving by a Convalescent in the Lydian Mode." This was written following his severe illness in the spring of 1825. The movement is in two sections; the first is a prayerful chorale and the second a more active section which represents, according to the composer, the feeling of the invalid regaining new strength. The entire quartet is indicative of his religious feeling and his gratitude for recovery from illness.

Haydn (1732-1809) arranged his orchestral work on the *Seven Last Words* for string quartet, and they were published in his quartet series as Op. 51.

Later writers of quartets have employed thematic material from prior sources. In 1896 *Prelude Religieux pour Instruments á cordes* by Charles Levade (1869-1948) was published in Paris. The one movement quartet *Quartet in C, Op. 46*, by David Stanley Smith (1877-1949) was played at the Berkshire Festival in 1921. He achieved purity of style using the Gregorian plainsong *Jesu Corona*. Gregorian illusions are found also in *Music for 4 Stringed Instruments* (1923) by Charles Loeffler (1861-1935). The second movement is said to be inspired by thoughts of Easter. It has been called both austere and touching music.

In addition to performance of string-quartet literature at church concerts and providing special music for festival occasions, the string quartet is valuable for accompaniment of cantatas and larger choral works. A quartet has rendered helpful assistance to a choir learning four-part a cappella works. The use of the string quartet with voices is excellent for both rehearsal and performance of Bach chorales. The *Concord Series No. 1* listed below is valuable training for either string players or vocalists or both.

A Selected List of String Quartet Literature for Church Use

(* *Especially suitable for students or amateurs*)

*Armstrong	Evening Prayer	C. Fischer
* Bach	Organ Preludes	C. Fischer
Arr. by H. Hodge	Set 1: Deck thyself, my soul, with gladness; Mortify us through thy Grace; I Cry to Thee, O Christ	
	Set 2: Come, Saviour of the Gentiles; Lord by thy Loving kindness; My Soul, Praise the Lord	
Bargiel	Andante Sostenuto from 1st Quartet in A Minor, Op. 15b	Associated Music Publishers
* Beethoven	Adagio Cantabile from Septet, Op. 20	C. Fischer
————	Adagio from Twelfth Quartet in E Flat, Op. 127	Peters
————	3rd movment, Song of Thanksgiving, from 15th Quartet, Op. 132	Peters
Cherubini	2nd movement, Larghetto sans lenteur, from First Quartet in E Flat	Peters
* Clarke, Irma	Concord Series No. 1 Twenty-five Bach Chorales	E. C. Schirmer
Franck	3rd movement, Larghetto, from D Major Quartet	Peters

27

* Froberger	Ricercare (1650)	Peters
* Haydn	Adagio from String Quartet, Op. 17, No. 1	C. Fischer
Loeffler	Music for 4 Stringed Instruments	C. Fischer (Society for the Publication of American Music)
* McLin, Edward	Chorales for Strings (30 easy chorales)	Pro-Art
Mendelssohn	Adagio from 5th Quartet, Op. 44, No. 3 in E Flat	Associated Music Publishers
————	3rd movement, Andante, from String Quartet, Op. 12	Hofmeister
Mozart	Andantino grazio from Quartet No. 22, K. 183	Peters
* Palestrina	8 Ricercari in Four Parts	E. C. Schirmer
* Pleyel, I.	Adagio from String Quartet, Op. 8, No. 1	Stainer & Bell
————	String Quartet No. 4 (Variations on Pleyel's Hymn)	Stainer & Bell
* Reiche, Gottfried	3 Sonatinas	E. C. Schirmer
Smith, D.	Quartet in C, Op. 46	C. Fischer (Society for the Publication of American Music)
Vivaldi Arr. by G. F. Chedini	3 Quartets (2 movements each) 1. Sinfonia Al Santo Sepolchro 2. Concerto Madrigalesco 3. Sonata Al Santo Sepolchro	International

Woodwind Ensembles

Historical accounts mention the use of oboes, bassoons, and courtals (an early bassoon) to support the voice parts in church choirs. An anthem written by Captain Cooke, a choirmaster of the Chapel Royal, Windsor, England, during the seventeenth century was described as being accompanied by "two double sackbuts and two double courtals placed at convenient distances amongst the classes of the gentlemen of both choirs, to the end that all might distinctly hear, and consequently keep together both in time and tune." [1]

In France André Campra (1660-1744), while director of music for the Cathedral of Notre Dame, combined orchestral instruments with the organ for choral accompaniments. In his setting of Psalm 126, *A Grand Choeur*, there are parts for two oboes and a bassoon, which not only duplicate the vocal parts but also contribute occasional obbligato accompaniments.

In Handel's *Chandos Anthems* organ and strings are employed, with one oboe, one bassoon, and sometimes two flutes. Bach (1685-1750) used the oboe as an obbligato instrument in many situations. He composed melodies for the oboe which seem to capture every mood and still challenge musicians. Bach was particularly fond of the oboe for obbligato parts to enhance arias for solo voice when the words of the text express lamentation or mournful sentiment.

[1] Orlando A. Mansfield, "Some Anomalies in Orchestral Accompaniments to Church Music," *Musical Quarterly*, II, 2 (April, 1916), 205.

Many interesting tales are told about the use of woodwind instruments in the village orchestras which were peculiar to the churches of English villages in earlier days. George Eliot, in *Scenes of Clerical Life*, colorfully reports the musical activity of bassoons: "On great occasions the choir sang an anthem in which the key-bugles always ran away at a great pace, while the bassoon every now and then boomed a flying shot after them." [2]

The Reverend Mr. John A. LaTrobe, an Anglican clergyman, writing in 1831 recounts what he feels is a description of a typical performance by a village orchestra that is more or less considered part of the choir.

Suppose a clergyman inducted to a country living, of which he comes to take possession. The small church is crowded to hear the "new parson," and the singers and performers are preparing in the gallery to make their best display. At the appointed time they commence. The first specimen he has of his choir is perhaps ushered in by a clarinet, which, though rather a favourite in country churches, is the most hapless in untutored hands. This is commissioned to lead off, and after some dreadful hiccups on the part of the instrument, which is its infirmity when clumsily dealt with, and which chases the blood chill through the veins, the tune is completed and the singing proceeds. Then other instruments are introduced—

the flute,
And the vile squeaking of the wry-necked fife,

[2] Gordon Anderson, "Some Old Church Instruments," *Monthly Musical Record*, XLVI (May 1, 1916), 141.

30

And it may be, breaking suddenly in with portentous thunder, after three or four notes spent in gathering up the long clambering instrument, some unlucky, deep-mouthed bassoon. It may readily be conceived, that these instruments by their united clamour, will lay a sufficient foundation of noise, upon which the singers may rear their superstructure. This they proceed to do with their whole breadth of lungs, each striving to surpass his neighbour in vociferation; till, exhausted with the exercise, they gradually cease, according to the tenure of their breath; the bassoon player, for the dignity of his instrument, commencing his last note rather later than the rest, and, by a peculiar motion of his shoulders, pumping out the whole power of his lungs in one prolonged and astounding roar. All sit down—a smile of self-gratulation playing about the lip, supposing that they have given their new parson a good idea of the manner in which they can anticipate the joys of heaven.[3]

Mr. LaTrobe continues with a passage on how much "courage, judgment, and forbearance" the new parson must use in reforming this musical performance. While there is always room for improvement in many areas, surely we can take pride in knowing that both church-music practices and music education have made some degree of improvement since 1831.

The early American usage of these instruments with church choirs is equally interesting. Many accounts are given of the necessity for their use, the suspicion they encountered, and how they overcame negativism

[3] *The Music of the Church* (London: L. B. Seeley & Sons, 1831), pp. 87-88.

toward their presence in church groups. In discussing reed instruments in churches Nathaniel Gould, whose *Church Music in America* was published in Boston in 1853, could not speak too well for the current performance on the oboe, or as he called it the "hautboy."

but the wind, being communicated through a delicate reed, required a correct ear, and a very considerable degree of skill, to manage it; also in unskilful hands, it was subject to squeaking and squalling; therefore, it did not receive very much favor or attention, but was looked upon as of doubtful character.[4]

Of the clarinet, which he says was introduced into the church next after the oboe, he said:

This instrument astonished every beholder, not so much, perhaps, on account of its sound, as its machinery. One that could manage the keys of a clarinet, forty-five years ago, so as to play a tune, was one of the wonders of the age. Children of all ages would crowd around the performer, and wonder and admire when the keys were moved.[5]

Concerning the bassoon he was able to speak more favorably:

After this [clarinet] came the bassoon. This was considered the climax of instruments for bass, coinciding so well with the human voice and bass-viol [cello] in church

---

[4] Boston: A. N. Johnson, 1853, p. 173.
[5] *Ibid.*

32

music, and having such power in a band of instruments, that for many years it had general favor.[6]

These descriptions are a long way from present performance ability on modern woodwinds. Instrumentalists today are highly capable of adding assistance to church services by aesthetic performance on oboe, clarinet, or bassoon. It will always be necessary to screen carefully the available literature for the instruments and to be certain that the music is of such a nature to add to rather than detract from the worship elements of the service.

The church music director will find the use of woodwind trios, quartets, or quintets can make desirable contributions to his program. Preparing woodwind ensembles for performance in the sanctuary demands attention to many musical factors and to several other fine details. In return the director will enjoy significant satisfaction for his delicate and thoroughly detailed efforts.

The woodwind quintet composed of flute, oboe, clarinet, horn, and bassoon offers five different tonal colors yet is capable of many interesting nuances and subtle blending of timbres. Beauty of tone for an ensemble composed of five instruments as diverse as those forming the woodwind quintet is achieved by systematic, consistent effort.

Just as in rehearsing a church choir, the director who

[6] *Ibid.*

coaches a woodwind quintet will want to do as much as possible to produce good tone quality, intonation, and balance. A good instrumentalist is accustomed to listening carefully to himself and to others while playing. Rehearsal of the quintet will commence, after a little individual warming of the instruments, with tuning to A-440. Next a few unison, or octave, scales will be helpful. Some rapid tonguing and dynamic changes can be made on scales. Bach chorales with flute and oboe on the top part are useful during this first part of the rehearsal. Then one should play a familiar piece before working on a new selection.

If at all possible each member of the ensemble should have had his music and studied—practiced—his part before the rehearsal. Ideally he will also have had a chance to read through the score so he will have some expectation of what other members will play, how his part relates to the other parts, and a rough idea of the composer's general intention. Ask each person to always bring a pencil to rehearsal in order to mark the parts for any nuances this particular ensemble desires to express.

The formation in which the members of a woodwind quintet are seated will affect audience receptivity. It is traditional for the flute to sit on the left of the audience. From this position the flutist can, when necessary, make gestures with his instrument for starting and stopping the group. One sees various plans for seating the other four players. This one plan is recommended particularly for good balance:

OBOE
BASSOON   CLARINET
FLUTE   HORN

It is particularly important, especially in a church sanctuary, to be certain that the horn player is not seated directly in front of a hard wall or directly in front of heavy drapes or paneling. The bell of his horn is sending the sound away from him as well as from his colleagues and the audience. The hard wall may give undesirable rebound, or drapes may absorb too much of the horn sound.

Playing in a woodwind ensemble, like any chamber music membership, is an enriching experience. Increased musical sensitivity is invariably a by-product. Coaching a woodwind ensemble is hard work but extraordinarily satisfying when the desired results are achieved.

Suggested literature for a newly organized quintet would be the collection of *Chorales and Motets* (Boston) and the Handel-Bauer *Six Little Fugues* (Broadcast Music, Inc.).

Music for Woodwind Ensembles

Woodwind Trios

Oboe or flute, clarinet	Bach (Hirsh)	I Call upon Thy Name, O Jesus	C. Fischer
Oboe, clarinet, bassoon	Bach (Oubradous)	Prelude et Fugue	Oiseau Lyre
Flute, clarinet, bassoon	Bach (Tarlow)	Fugue in C Minor	Elkan Vogel
2 clarinets, bassoon	Bach (Thurston)	Three Fugues	Boosey & Hawkes
3 clarinets	Beethoven	Adagio Cantabile from Trio, Op. 2	Cundy-Bettoney
clarinet, bassoon, piano	Glazunof	Trio Pathetique	Jurgenson

35

Woodwind Quartets

flute or oboe, clarinet, horn, bassoon	Bach (Hirsh)	Fugue in E Flat	C. Fischer
4 clarinets	Bach (Holmes)	Grant us to do with zeal	Rubank
2 clarinets, 2 bassoons	Bach (Trinkaus)	O Sacred Head	G. Schirmer
3 flutes, alto flute (or clarinet or horn)	Jongen, J.	2 Paraphrases on Walloon Christmas Carols	Southern Music
4 clarinets	Mozart (Voxman)	Ave Verum Corpus	Rubank
Flute, oboe, clarinet, bassoon	Scarlatti (Rocereto)	Pastorale in F	Volkwein

Woodwind Quintets

(Flute, Oboe, Clarinet, Horn, Bassoon)

Bach	Sarabande in D Minor	Breitkopf-Hartel
Bach (Barrere)	Sonatina from Gottes Zeit	G. Schirmer
Bach (Hirsh)	Fugue in C Minor	Ditson
Bach (Lake)	Collection of Chorales	G. Schirmer
Beach, Mrs. H.	Pastorale	Composer's Press
Beethoven (Barrere)	Adagio, Op. 71	G. Schirmer
Borch	Sunrise on the Mountains	Belwin
Desportes, Y.	Prelude and Pastorale	Southern Music
———	Prelude, variations and finale on a Gregorian Chant	Baron
Handel (Bauer)	Six Little Fugues	Broadcast Music, Inc.
Liszt (Seay)	Weihnachtslied	Jack Spratt
Mendelssohn	Figurate Hymn	C. Fischer
Mozart (Cailliet)	Quintet in F	Elkan Vogel
Persichetti	Pastoral, Op. 21	G. Schirmer
Pfeiffer, G.	Pastorale	Southern Music
Pierné, G.	Pastorale, Op. 14, No. 1	Leduc

Sodero	Morning Prayer	Associated Music Publishers
Collection	Chorales & Motets	Boston

String and Wind Music for Christmas

During the Christmas season it is appropriate to offer concerts in the church. If a church does not have an orchestra or does not have instrumental performers available, the director of music may consider the possibility of inviting a school or college group to present a concert or to assist in planning and presenting a program. Our heritage of music literature has not only a wealth of choral materials composed to celebrate the birth of Christ, but also a number of excellent instrumental works.

Among the orchestral works written for use in church services or in sacred concerts are Christmas concerti—in concerto grosso style—by early Italian composers. Frequently the first or last movement is a pastorale with a quiet melody in 6/8 or 12/8 meter. Technically these pieces are not very difficult but they are important music literature. Noble in concept, these works came from a period in music history—the latter part of the seventeenth and first part of the eighteenth century—during which the patronage of instrumental music rivaled that of vocal music.

Arcangelo Corelli inscribed his *Concerto Grosso in G Minor, Op. 6, No. 8* (Peters), *Fatto per la notte di natale*, "made for the night of the nativity." Written for the usual concertino of two violins and cello with

37

string orchestra and continuo, this work is a tuneful, dignified masterpiece.

Giuseppi Torelli (ca. 1650-1708) is thought to have patterned his *Christmas Concerto, Op. 8* (Associated Music Publishers) after Corelli's. It is a charming work written for two violins, string orchestra, and continuo.

If only a few string players are available perhaps *Weinachts Pastorale* by Giuseppi Valentini (1681-1740) can be played. It was originally written for two violins, bass, and cembalo. A modern edition by Arnold Schering is for two violins, cello, and piano *ad lib.* (Associated Music Publishers) This work is quite easy but well worth performing. There is also an arrangement for string orchestra.

Another concerto grosso by an eighteenth-century Italian, Francesco Manfredini (1680-1748), uses two obligato violins, string orchestra, and continuo. In this *Christmas Concerto* (Associated Music Publishers) the pastorale is the first of three movements. The second movement is an expressive largo, and the finale is allegro.

Handel's *Pastoral Symphony* from *Messiah* is available in several arrangements. Mozart originally scored it for three violins, viola, and bass, but added eight woodwinds and two horns to the orchestra. Additional Christmas selections for string orchestra are:

Bach	Overture to Christmas Cantata	Volkwein
Brahms	Es ist ein Ros' entsprungen	Oxford
Niemann	Hirtenmusik zur Weihnacht	Peters

(available for rental
only)

Willan	Chorale Prelude on Puer	Concordia
	nobis nascitur	

Some of the music mentioned above has been published in excellent arrangements for brass ensembles. The festive nature of Christmas lends itself especially to the use of brass ensembles. There are many materials listed in Chapters IV and V that are appropriate and more churchly than the potpourri type of Christmas medleys.

If your church has woodwind players available here are some suggestions of appropriate Christmas repertoire. Floyd O. Harris has made a good harmonic arrangement of Amanda Kennedy's well-known *Star of the East* for three flutes (Ludwig). This is especially appropriate to accompany a Christmas pageant in pantomime. There is also the *Christmas Pastorale* by Vivaldi (McGinnis and Marx) which is an arrangement of a larghetto movement from the *Il Pastore Fido* set of sonatas, to be played by flute, cello, and organ. For flute, violin, and a keyboard instrument there is *Noel Allemand*, a concerto with three movements—allegro, adagio, allegro. This is based on the old German hymn *Lobt Gott, ihr Christen, allzugleich* (Presto).

For Christmas music of a delicate nature try Harald Rohlig's *A Little Shepherd Music* for organ with flute, oboe, clarinet or recorder (Concordia). There are several selections for recorders that are appropriate for the

39

Christmas season. *Christmas Pastorale* by Robin Milford (Oxford) is a delightful piece for alto recorder and piano. William Appleby's *Christmas Suite* (Oxford) for soprano recorder, violin, and cello is also interesting. A. W. Benoy has arranged several collections of carols for recorder ensembles (Oxford).

These are only a few of the many usable portions of music literature available to enhance the festive nature of the Christmas season in your church. Be sure to plan early to enlist the aid of the string and wind players in your church for special Christmas programs.

CHAPTER IV

Small Ensembles: Brass

Trumpets

For centuries the sound of the trumpet has been used to praise God. Before monotheism became prevalent trumpets were used in religious rites by primitive peoples.

Josephus, a Jewish historian, describes the two trumpets God instructed Moses to make (See Numbers 10) as tubes a little less that a cubit in length and somewhat thicker than flutes, of pure silver with rather elongated bells and producing a shrill, distinct sound. Under the authority of Moses the blowing of these trumpets was a function reserved for the priests.

Both books of Chronicles record the sounding of trumpets in connection with worship and the rejoicing of the people. Singing with wind instrument accompaniment has a biblical heritage: "And it was the duty of the trumpeters and singers to make themselves heard in unison in praise and thanksgiving to the Lord" (II Chr. 5:13). Josephus also states that 200,000 silver trumpets were used in the great temple of Solomon at Jerusalem.

Other biblical references to the trumpet are numerous. In each instance its use was related to an event of great importance.

During the Middle Ages kings and noblemen enjoyed exclusive right to use the trumpet for religious and ceremonial occasions. In 1620 when J. H. Schein (1586-1630), one of Bach's predecessors at Leipzig, chose trumpets and timpani for his setting of Psalm 150 for a wedding of common citizens he was taken to task by the Saxon court.

During this period in France trumpets were also used in the Roman Mass to augment the ceremony of the consecration of the host. The people were required to observe the consecrated wafer. When the priest raised up the host so it could be seen by all the people the dramatic moment was enhanced by the sound of trumpets.

During the latter part of the seventeenth century and the beginning of the eighteenth century Italian church musicians produced many instrumental works for the church. The Bologna School especially produced serious works for trumpet and string orchestra. Michael Praetorius (1517-1621), a German student of Italian methods, enjoyed filling the church with instrumental sound. The sounds emanating from the trumpets of his time, however, were not as easily blended as those of our modern instruments. In the third book of his *Syntagma Musicum* he explained how certain of his concerti were to be performed. He desired that five, six, or seven trumpeters be stationed in a special place outside the church in order that the loud sounds would not deafen the musicians within.

By 1768 no less person than Wolfgang Mozart (1756-91) was commissioned to compose a trumpet concerto to be performed before the court, the occasion being the dedication of a new orphanage in Vienna.

Trumpets of former times were difficult to play with good tone and intonation. Today, however, with a long and illustrious history, the trumpet is a refined instrument capable of being played with beautiful tone and excellent intonation. Trumpet teachers in our schools and colleges are preparing students with adequate technique and musicianship worthy of performance in our churches. The list of music following demonstrates the availability of a usable body of literature. In addition to the music listed, descants to hymns are highly recommended for trumpets. Such a descant provides a striking climax for a hymn festival or for a festival service.

The chorale concertatos represent exceptionally fine use of the combination of organ, choir, congregation, and instruments. Paul Bunjes' concertato on "A mighty fortress is our God" was prepared to enrich a Reformation festival service. It consists of a chorale for organ alone followed by stanza one, the congregation singing in unison with organ. Stanza two is for mixed chorus. The third stanza uses three trumpets with organ and the congregation in unison. Stanza four also uses organ and congregation but adds a treble descant and two trumpet parts, one in unison with the melody, the other in unison with the descant. Trumpet and choir parts are available separately.

The chorale concertato listed by Harald Rohlig is

for choir, congregation, flute, trumpet, and organ. This is splendid material with no special difficulties. It begins with an intrada and chorale for trumpet and organ followed by stanza one of the hymn for choir and organ. A ritornello for flute and organ is followed by stanza two sung by the congregation and a junior choir. Stanza three is a pastorale for organ. The choir sings the fourth stanza a cappella, and another ritornello for flute and organ follows. All forces unite for the last stanza, with the choir singing countermelodic alleluias.

Music for Trumpets

Trumpet and Strings

Hovhaness	Prayer of Saint Gregory	Robert King
Torelli	Sinfonia con Tromba	Robert King

Two Trumpets and SATB

Cassler	Now Let the Vault of Heaven Resound	Augsburg

Three Trumpets and Organ

Bach	Now Thank We All Our God	Robert King
Buxtehude	Fanfare and Chorus	Robert King
Karg-Elert	Nun Danket Alle Gott	Robert King
Lassus	Providebam Dominum	Robert King

Three Trumpets, Timpani, and Organ

Bach	Two Fanfares and Chorale	Robert King

Three Trumpets and SATB

Hannahs	Hosanna to the Son of David	H. W. Gray

Three Trumpets, Timpani, and SATB

Coke-Jephcott	Variants for Saint Anne	H. W. Gray

Four Trumpets

Mozart (Ostrander)	Alleluja	Brodt

44

| Trowbridge | Chorale for Four Trumpets | Henri Elkan |
| Whistler and Hummel | Chorale Classics: A Collection for Band | Rubank |

Four Trumpets and Piano

| Purcell (Ostrander) | Sound the Trumpets | Brodt |

Three Trumpets, Organ, Chorus

| Bunjes | A Mighty Fortress Is Our God | Concordia |

Trumpet, Organ, Chorus

Bunjes	All Praise to God Who Reigns Above	Concordia
————	I Know That My Redeemer Lives	Concordia
————	Praise to the Lord, the Almighty	Concordia

Trumpet, Flute, Organ, Chorus

| Rohlig | Praise to the Lord, the Almighty | Concordia |

French Horns

One hears horns in churches in brass groups and in woodwind quintets, and occasionally a horn solo is played. Although the trombone and trumpet appear to have a more specific historical background in church usage the modern horn is extremely will suited to perform in the church. In the hands of an able performer the quality of horn tone ranges from brilliant to a mellowed darkness. The horn has countless moods and emotions within its potential. Many writers have attempted to describe the rapturous appeal of the horn. Its tone color can be distant and mysterious when played with hand muting. It may be mellow or ro-

45

mantic, and when called upon to do so it can sound heroic, or even sinister if desired. With this seemingly endless variety of tone colors at his command a skilled hornist derives tremendous satisfaction from discovering the refined musical expression that he can portray on his instrument.

The first horns used in religious services were probably those made from the horns of animals. However ancient civilizations also knew the art of working metals. Various uses are reported for early horns. Ulph, the son-in-law of King Canute of England, started a custom that led to the use of horns as a title to land or property. At the communion altar he drank wine from his horn, then dedicated all his lands to God and to Peter. Now in the treasury of York Minster this horn is the proof that certain estates belong to the Church.

Horns played for the hunt developed certain traditions. As they increased in length it became necessary to coil them. Shortly after this they were introduced into the orchestra. Yet even in the time of Handel they were played with bells turned up and the sound produced was a blare. At first the horns were used in the orchestra primarily to depict hunting scenes for operas. Bach, with his usual precise effort to indicate tone colors, uses a coiled horn—*corno da caccia*, also called *Jägdhorn*—with the bass aria *Quoniam tu solus Dominus* of the *Hohe Messe*. Bach's acknowledgment of the sovereignty of Christ is reinforced by a florid part played by this horn. The instrumentation of

Cantata No. 143, Lobe den Herrn, meine seele, includes three *corni di caccia.*

The French horn as we know it today is a quite modern instrument. The first double horn, the type now prevalent, was not made until 1900. Only a few years ago the horn parts in music played by an average school band or orchestra were dull both harmonically and rhythmically. Today the horns are an important part of these school music groups, and interesting parts are being written for them along with an increased number of solos and ensembles.

The sound of a quartet of horns can give a great deal of aesthetic satisfaction to both performers and listeners. A music director cannot usually just put four horns together and immediately produce a beautiful horn-quartet sound. Many hours of work by the four together, preferably with a good coach, are necessary to insure adequate intonation and the required feeling of ensemble. It is well worth the effort, however, and there are a number of very good quartets for church use, with every expectation of more on their way to being published.

Music for Horn Quartet
(Four French Horns)

Bach (Treat)	Fugue in B Flat	Remick
Bizet (Zamecvik)	Agnus Dei	Sam Fox
Godard (Holmes)	Adagio Pathetique	Barnhouse
Graham, W.	Minaret	Pro-Art

47

Griend	Horn Quartet	Donemus (Amsterdam, 1945)
Handel Arr. by D'Arese	Largo	C. Fischer
Lorenz-Pottag	Adagio Religioso	Belwin
McKay, F.	Molto Religioso (from Divertimento, Op. 16)	C. Fischer
Mozart (Ostrander)	Alleluia	Editions Musicus
Palestrina (Schultz)	Lux Vera	Kendor
Vittoria (Schultz)	O Sacrum Convivium	Kendor

Trombones

Martin Luther's translation of the Bible uses the German word posaune (trombone) for ceremonial occasions, reserving the trumpet for military occasions. For Luther it is the archangel's trombone that will sound at the day of judgment.

The sixteenth century trombone can be seen in various pictures. The bell was smaller and less flaring, and the instrument was made of thicker material than modern trombones. Consequently, because its sound was somewhat mellow, it blended well with voices and string instruments and was frequently used in churches. At the beginning of the seventeenth century many composers of church music were still writing concerti and canzoni for instrumental ensembles composed of violins and trombones. Even before this trombones had been used in their own right without strings.

48

"There are still extant some very fine specimens of four-part chorales, with a simple organ accompaniment, round which are grouped from four to six trombone-parts of wonderfully rich construction, winding themselves round the choral parts like a highly coloured garland." [1]

Heinrich Schütz (1585-1672) included two works for bass voice with four trombones in his *Symphoniae Sacrae*: *Fili mi, Absalom,* and *Attendite, popule meus, legem meam* (with continuo). Daniel Speer (1636-1707) wrote a sonata for four trombones and continuo.

Early trombones were manufactured in choirs, soprano, alto, tenor, and bass. Beethoven's *Three Equali* composed in 1812 for a trombone quartet was played at Gladstone's funeral in Westminster Abbey in 1898. A writer who was present said: "The hushed stillness which pervaded the noble fane was broken with indescribable tenderness as the sustained chord of D minor fell upon the ears of the great congregation in tones of weird simplicity and exquisite pathos." [2]

This important, uncomplicated music is now available in an edition for brass choir, as well as an edition for a quartet of trombones.

Early American use of brass instruments in church services was pioneered by the Moravians. In 1754 a set of four trombones—soprano, alto, tenor, and bass —was imported from Europe for the use of the Mo-

[1] J. A. Kappey, *Military Music* (London: Boosey & Company, 1894), p. 55

[2] Mansfield, *op. cit.* p. 208.

ravian Church at Bethlehem, Pennsylvania. Other trombones were added later. The trombone choir played at all festivals and funerals. Rufus A. Grider describing music in Bethlehem said:

The trombones were used on Festal occasions—to announce the Festival from the church steeple, the time being about seven and half o'clock a.m., again at the opening of service, at the love feast at two o'clock p.m. and at night, (if open air meetings are held) as upon the occasion of the Children's Festival. The tunes are varied to suit the occasion.[3]

A set of trombones was imported for a North Carolina congregation, and they were first played at Bethabara, the oldest Moravian settlement in the South, in 1765. Roberta Bitgood emphasizes that the traditional trombone choirs had nothing to do with the various town bands that flourished.

It was always devoted to ecclesiastical music, connected with inspiring and solemn religious festivals. The members had to be ready and willing to be called to the belfry of the church at any hour of any day to pour down on the morning or evening stillness, or upon the mid-day bustle and noise of the streets, the mellow strains of the significant three chorales, and then to serve a few days later to accompany the sequel of what those tunes from the belfry

[3] Quoted by Roberta Bitgood, "Music in the Moravian Church in America" (Master's thesis, School of Sacred Music, Union Theological Seminary, 1935), p. 40. Used by permission of Roberta Bitgood.

told listeners at a new made grave in "God's Acre" with which thoughts most holy and memories exceeding tender are associated. The playing was an act of devotion to the church and it was not always pleasant or easy. In cold weather the moisture would congeal in the instruments, making it almost impossible to play.[4]

The story is told that in 1758 the lives of those at Bethlehem were saved by the trombone music. Indians were prowling around the settlement waiting until near daybreak to set fire to the place. The music of the trombones announced the Festal Day at 4:00 A.M. and frightened them away. The Indians believed that the Great Spirit must be hovering near the place guarding it from harm.

The Moravian Trombone Choir still functions and takes part in the yearly festival of the Bach Choir at Bethlehem. Ruth Scott describes the work of the trombone choir on Easter:

But most important, the Trombone Choir is the characteristic, the indispensable feature of the Moravian celebration of Resurrection Day. Sometime after midnight on Easter morning, the Bethlehem choir starts from the Central Church and travels about the city, playing Easter chorales on street corners in various sections. At 5:15 they are back at the church where, from the rear of the organ loft, they announce the opening chorale of the Easter Morning Liturgy. After the short church service, the trombonists lead the choir and the congregation up the hill-

---

[4] *Ibid.*, pp. 53-54.

side to the cemetery and accompany the sung parts of the service there.[5]

As a result of a Protestant revival started in Germany in 1843 many trombone choirs developed in Germany. Although called trombone choirs they used keyed bugles on the top parts and today use various combinations of brass instruments. These choirs were developed to lead group singing of an evangelistic nature. Their entire repertoire consisted of religious songs because the leadership of this movement felt that music with words was more likely to stimulate the faith and produce converts and that by this method the instruments could preach the Word of God. Many of these choirs are still in existence. Recent information indicates that changes in both instrumentation and repertoire have begun.

Today we have fine music available and a most splendid heritage of the use of trombones in churches and religious services.

Music for Trombone Ensembles

Two Trombones with Piano

Briegel	Cathedral Echoes	Briegel
Liddle	How Lovely Are Thy Dwellings	Boosey & Hawkes
Thome-Traxler	Andante Religioso	Belwin

Two Trombones with Organ

| Strauss, R. | Festival Procession | Peters |

[5] Ruth Scott, "Music Among the Moravians" (Master's thesis, Eastman School of Music, 1938), p. 70. Used by permission of Ruth Scott Bird.

Three Trombones

Anonymous Ed. by R. King	Two Medieval Motets	Robert King
Beethoven (Ostrander)	Suite from the Mount of Olives	Robert King
Handel (Ostrander)	Suite	Robert King
Mozart (Ostrander)	Suite	Robert King
Stieber, H.	Turmmusik No. 2	Robert King
Uber, David	The Cloisters	Editions Musicus

Four Trombones

Bach	Sixteen Chorales	Robert King
Beethoven	Equali for Trombones	Robert King
Berlioz (Ostrander)	The Stable at Bethlehem	Editions Musicus
Bizet (Briegel)	Agnus Dei	Briegel
Busch, C.	Meditation	C. Fischer
———	Quietude	C. Fischer
Costa (Arr. E. Irons)	I Will Extol Thee	Rubank
Franck (Stube)	Panis Angelicus	Belwin
Fuss	25 Ernste and Religiose Stüke	Robert King
Godard-Holmes	Adagio Pathetique	Barnhouse
Haubiel	Recessional	Composers Press
Hurrell	Two Chorales	Briegel
Johnson, C.	Prelude Solemnelle	FitzSimons
McCarty, P.	Recitative and Fugue	Robert King
Scheidt, S.	Da Jesus an dem Kreuze Stund	Robert King
King, R. (ed.)	24 Early German Chorales	Robert King
Traditional Arr. by N. Long	Favorite Festival Carols	Volkwein

Trombone in Chamber Music

Biber Ed. by K.	Sonata a tre (Trombone, 2 violins, and	Musica Rara London,

53

Janetzky	continuo)	1958
Hovhaness	Concerto No. 3	American
	Diran, the Religious Singer	Composers
	(Trombone and Strings)	Alliance,
		New York,
		1949

Trombone with Voices

Bruckner	Two Motets: Offertorium, Ecce sacerdos	Peters
	(Mixed Voices and 3 trombones [with organ])	
Jacobson, G.	Sombre Suite in five movements	Jacobson, 1951
	(Trombone, alto, clarinet, viola)	Mss. obtainable from author: College of Emporia, Emporia, Kansas
Schütz	Absalom, Fili Mi	King
	(Latin and English)	

Brass Quartet, Quintet, Sextet

Numerous churches today use brass quartets on occasion, and in at least one church, the Cathedral Church of St. Paul in Boston, a brass quartet plays every Sunday in the year.

There are many ways in which a small brass ensemble may be used effectively in worship services. The ensemble may play alone or with organ for preludes, interludes, and postludes, thus lending a joyous dignity to the service. The brass may also play alone or with organ to accompany the congregation in all or in selected stanzas of hymns. They may play in unison and octaves to re-inforce the melody while the organist

54

plays a free harmonization, or trombones may play the melody and the trumpets a descant for a final climactic stanza. For a festival processional the ensemble may provide interludes between stanzas. In these ways a brass group provides increased motivation for congregational hymn singing.

Many anthems, especially those of a festival nature, are written with parts for brass ensembles or optional brass. Used antiphonally from a rear or side gallery the quartet is especially effective.

Easter Day and Christmas musical services are choice occasions to use a brass ensemble outside the church, playing from the steps or a roof or tower location to welcome worshipers as they approach the sanctuary. Appropriate hymns, carols, and Bach chorales are especially effective on such occasions.

Worship services held outdoors often suffer from lack of a good musical instrument. This is frequently true at summer campsites. Here the brass quartet can be a valuable asset, playing for the entire service.

The use of a brass quartet, or other ensemble, in worship should be announced in the bulletin to help the congregation prepare for the experience. Members of the congregation should be led to realize that they are vital participants in this expression of praise.

When a brass ensemble is to play in the service it is important that every detail be thoroughly planned and rehearsed in advance. Locating the group for best acoustical and worship results, balance with choir and organ, use of music and music stands, robing, entrances—these mechanics should be so well planned that they do not detract from the service. A few suggestions of literature for church use follow.

Music for Small Brass Ensembles

Brass Trio (2 cornets or trumpets and trombone)

Ehmann	Evangelisches Kantoreibuch (Church year chorale collection)	Robert King
Ostrander, A.	Suite for Three Brass Instruments	Editions Musicus

Brass Quartet (2 cornets or trumpets, 2 trombones or one trombone, one baritone)

Bach	Chorale from Christmas Oratorio	Rubank
————	Prelude and Fugue in D	Edward B. Marks
————	Triumphant Rose the Son of God	Rubank
Bach (Post)	Agnus Dei	Editions Musicus
Banchieri	Sinfonia	C. Fischer
Beethoven	Nature's Praise of God	Rubank
Beethoven (Kahn)	Three Equale	Edward B. Marks
Gabrieli	Canzona per Sonare, Nos. 1, 2, 3,	Robert King
Gabrieli (Smith)	Ricercare	Brodt
Glazunov	In Modo Religioso	Robert King
Haydn	Spacious Firmament on High	Rubank
Law-Hewitt-Billings	Three New England Hymns	Robert King
Mendelssohn	Faith, Op. 102, No. 6	Briegel
Mozart	Fugue	Robert King
Norden	A Solemne Musick	Brodt
Pachelbel	Two Magnificats	Robert King
Palestrina	Ricercar del Primo Tuono	Robert King
————	Three Hymns	Robert King

56

Tenaglia-Cheyette	Aria	Brodt
Reformation		
Chorales		Robert King

Brass Quartet and Organ

Bach	Alleluia from Christmas Cantata	Robert King
————	In Dulci Jubilo	Robert King
————	Jesu, nun sei gepreiset	Robert King
Bonelli	Toccata	Robert King
Brahms	O Welt, ich muss dich Lassen	Robert King
Gabrieli	Canzon Noni Toni	Brodt
King	Prelude and Fugue	Robert King
Marcello, B.	First Movement from Psalm XIX	Robert King
————	The heavens are telling	Robert King
Pachelbel	Allein Gott in der höh sei ehr	Robert King

Brass Quartet, Timpani, SATB Chorus

Broughton	Easter Paean	H. W. Gray
————	Easter Song	H. W. Gray
————	Hail, Festal Day	H. W. Gray
Dickinson	An Easter Litany	H. W. Gray
Liszt (Dickinson)	Easter Song of the Angels	H. W. Gray
Liszt (Dickinson)	The Resurrection	H. W. Gray
Nagler (Dickinson)	Hail, Thou Glorious Easter Day	H. W. Gray

Brass Quartet with SATB

Des Prez	Absalom, fili mi	Robert King
Dickinson	Resurrection Morn	H. W. Gray
————	All Hail the Virgin's Son	H. W. Gray
Neff	Four Traditional Carols	Summy-Birchard
Praetorius	In Dulci Jubilo	Robert King
Purcell	Music for Queen Mary II	Robert King

Brass Quintet (2 cornets or trumpets, horn, trombone, and tuba)

Bach, (Arr. W. Beeler)	Contrapunctus IX from Art of Fugue	Mentor Music

	If Thou Be Near	Rubank
(Arr. J. Glasel)		
Hobbs, Charles M.	Chorale for Sunrise (3 cornets, 2 trombones)	Canyon
Tufili, W.	A Prayer (2 trumpets, horn, baritone, trombone)	Pro-Art

Brass Sextet (2 trumpets, horn, trombone, baritone, tuba)

Borowski	Twilight Hymn	Boosey & Hawkes
Franck (Trinkaus)	Panis Angelicus	EMB
Haubiel	Ballade for Brass Sextet	Composers Press
Méhul	Joseph in Egypt	C. Fischer
Rosenmuller (Busch)	Prelude and Choral	C. Fischer
Wagner (Trinkaus)	Prayer from Rienzi	Witmark

CHAPTER V

Large Ensembles

Brass Choirs

During the Middle Ages each European town guarded its safety from predatory feudal lords by keeping watchmen in high towers or in the church steeples. Signals by wind instruments warned of an approaching enemy or of a fire. In some towns these watchmen also sounded a signal each hour in lieu of a town clock. Gradually the custom of playing harmonized chorales for this purpose developed. The "tower men" would perform a sacred tune at daybreak. After the Reformation a chorale was played with *zinken* and trombones at morning, noon, and evening to remind the people to say their prayers.

Municipal musicians formed brotherhoods, or guilds, in order to keep the vagabonds, or wandering minstrels, from infringing on their income by playing at local events such as weddings and festival occasions. The documents that these early guild members were required to sign were designed to gain the favor of both church and municipal authorities. The musician signed a paper to the effect that he would be a good Christian and endeavor to be a good citizen. He also agreed to attend the annual Court of Minstrels held on the Day of Assumption. Preceded by a worship service, a court consisting of a jury of elected superior musicians heard disputes, and a steward gave a "charge" emphasizing that the purpose of all music, both string and wind, was to praise and glorify God.

In the city of Leipzig chorales were sounded by tower men from three churches at 3:30 A.M., 11:00 A.M., and in the evening as the town gates were closed. Another group known as *stadtpfeifer* performed each morning at ten from a balcony of city hall. Different procedures were followed in different cities. In Berlin the *stadtpfeifer* were also the tower men. They performed chorales twice a day, at 10:00 A.M., and at 9:00 or 10:00 P.M. depending on the season of the year. The church calendar indicated the chorale to be played. At Christmastime *In dulci Jubilo* was played. At Easter the chorale was *Christ ist erstanden*. When a citizen died chorales were played from the church tower for his funeral.

Various instruments were used by tower men. There were trombones, fifes, oboes, *zinken*, drums, and in later years, horns. Trumpets were not yet used as they were exclusively the right of kings and nobles for religious and ceremonial uses.

In England the municipal musicians were called waits. They were to attend the mayor and the aldermen to and from church and play at festivals. Describing the waits of Norwich, William Kemp wrote in 1599:

Such Waytes (under Benedicitie be it spoken) few citties in the Realme haue the like, none better; who besides their excellency in wind instruments, their rare cunning on the Vyoll and Violin, theyre voices be admirable, euerie one of them able to serue in any Cathedrall Church in Christendome for Quiresters.[1]

For the tower musician a considerable amount of music was necessary for each day's performance. The church music of the period furnished good examples of polyphonic composition for these musicians who participated in religious festivals. Much of the original tower music is not now available, perhaps because apprentices learned by rote from their masters. Gradually customs and traditions in instrumentation and the playing of special tower compositions emerged. Two famous composers of tower music were Johann Pezel (1639-94) and Gottfried Reiche.

Pezel's music is found mainly in two collections: *Hora Decima*, to be played at 10:00 A.M., and *Funff-stimmigte blasende Musik*. The first, published in Leipzig in 1670, consisted of forty sonatas for two cornetti and three trombones. Most of the sonatas have only two movements. The second collection, published in Frankfurt in 1685, has seventy-six compositions, forty of which are called intrada. Pezel's music is straightforward, dignified, and excellently suited for brass ensembles. While most selections are not too difficult for young players, professional musicians are

[1] Quoted by Frank Kidson in *Grove's Dictionary of Music and Musicians* (3rd ed.; New York: The Macmillan Company, 1927), V, 612.

still proud to play them. This music is valuable for educational purposes as well as performance.

Gottfried Reiche, who played trumpet and other instruments in J. S. Bach's Leipzig church orchestra, was a member of the *stadtpfeifer* from 1706 until his death in 1723. His collection of twenty-four tower sonatas, *Neue Quatricinia*, published in 1696 is for one cornett and three trombones. (The cornett was an instrument made of wood and covered with leather. It had a chromatic range of at least two octaves and was widely used in church music.) He inscribed it, "Industriously composed to honor the Highest God and for the use and pleasure of musicians." Many of the compositions are fugues on abstract subjects. They are satisfying to play and rewarding to the listener. There is a sense of peace and nobility about them.

While this tower music was popular others were also putting wind instruments to use in religious music. English cathedrals were using cornetts and sackbuts (trombones) at least as early as 1532. Churches in France and Belgium were also using these instruments.

Andrea Gabrieli (ca. 1520-86), Adrian Willaert (ca. 1490-1562), and Giovanni Gabrieli (ca. 1557-1612) introduced instrumental parts with choral works at St. Mark's Cathedral in Venice. G. Gabrieli pioneered in designating specific instrumentation and developed compositions with full orchestrations. His *Surrexit Christus* includes some selections for instruments alone. These purely instrumental works for church use are the forerunners of the sonata and the symphony.

Gabrieli's canzoni, among the first works for instrumental ensembles alone, have been transcribed for modern brass ensembles in delightful editions.

Brass ensembles or brass choirs are splendid vehicles for special worship services. There is appropriate music available from both historic and contemporary sources. The following program performed by a college brass choir shows the use of music for brass alone as a medium for a special worship service. (For a discussion of brasses with voices see page 68.)

AN EVENING WORSHIP SERVICE
(For Brass Choir and a Narrator)
Theme: Christian Characteristics

1. One of the characteristics of a Christian person is that the Christian has a definite faith. In the Protestant tradition we have expressed some of the characteristics of a Christian through our hymns. Hymns and chorales have a long and illustrious association with performance by brass instruments. As we play Martin Luther's chorale "A mighty fortress is our God," will you sing with us this particular statement of our faith.

BRASS CHOIR: "A mighty fortress is our God"

2. The Christian is a thankful person. This is shown in the attitude toward God and man. A Christian remembers to thank God. Sing with us another well-known hymn: "Now thank we all our God."

63

BRASS CHOIR: "Now thank we all our God"

3. These chorales you have sung came from a period of history during which religion was uppermost in the daily lives of most of the people. European towns maintained town towers, and musicians performed wind music from these towers at various hours of the day reminding people to engage in prayers. Many pieces of music composed for use by these municipal musicians exemplify the solemnity and dignity of a stabilized faith.

Gottfried Reiche inscribed the title page for his tower sonatas, "Industriously composed to honor the Highest God and for the use and pleasure of musicians." While we play Reiche's *Sonata No. 7* will you meditate with us on the stable, yet dynamic, nature of our Christian faith.

BRASS CHOIR: Reiche, *Sonata No. 7*

4. Not only is the Christian a stable person with a stable faith, but he is also one who couples the respect he has for God and man with an exuberance for living. It was said of Henry Purcell's church music that it was to be noted and approved by man as well as for the glory of God. As you listen to Purcell's *March and Canzona* note the expression of serious respect followed by a sober, yet basically happy, feeling.

64

BRASS CHOIR: Purcell, *March and Canzona*

5. The Christian is a devout person. The attitude of prayer is natural to him. It is necessary both because a Christian is thankful and happy and because he also knows suffering and struggle. We will play a devotional hymn by Palestrina. Please assume the attitude of prayer and remain in this attitude at the close of the hymn.

BRASS CHOIR: Palestrina, *Surgentum cum Victoria*

6. Let us pray. (Prayer in keeping with theme of program)

7. Sometimes people have thought, because of some person's preoccupation with the foregoing characteristics, that the religious person is mentally cloistered, overly busy with his religion or likely to become wholly concerned with suffering. For the Christian suffering is not primary, however. Only the ability to endure it gracefully and to let it form a background for true joy is important. When the report came to King David that his son Absalom had been killed in battle he was deeply grieved. "Absalom, my son" has been a favorite text for composers who wished to express poignant sorrow. The brass choir will play a fifteenth century motet. The words are translated, "O Absalom, my son, would that I might die for thee, that I live no longer, but descend weeping into the everlasting dwelling."

65

BRASS CHOIR: Josquin des Prez, *Absalom, fili mi*

8. A sense of joy exists for all who are Christians. To illustrate the feeling of Christian joy we will play Gabrieli's *La Spiritata*. The title of this composition indicates a light, joyous nature. It was composed specifically for use in a church, St. Mark's Cathedral in Venice, near the beginning of the seventeenth century.

BRASS CHOIR: G. Gabrieli, *La Spiritata*

9. The joyous happy spirit of a Christian person can be recognized by the enthusiasm he brings to contemporary affairs. He is not buried in the past. He is active today and looking forward to the future. Having been created in the image of God, it is natural for the Christian to create new forms, to envision new styles, to permit his free spirit spontaneity. Spontaneity does not indicate lack of control but rather a particular way of organizing ideas. For many years church organists have practiced the creative art of improvisation.

BRASS CHOIR: Example of improvisation and modulation

10. Showing the seriousness of contemporary composers for brass groups the brass choir now plays the *Prelude and Fugue* by Robert King.

BRASS CHOIR: King, *Prelude and Fugue*

11. We have tried to indicate through music a few of the characteristics essential for Christian persons and to provide through this music a little time for meditation. During the playing of the postlude please feel free to leave—or to stay if you wish.

BRASS CHOIR: (Postlude) G. Gabrieli, *Canzona No. 4*

Brass Choir Music

(All this list is from the catalog of Robert King. Typical instrumentation is for two trumpets, horn, trombone, baritone or trombone, and tuba. See catalog for exact instrumentation on each selection. Although much of the music can be played with less, I recommend a minimum group of six cornets or trumpets, three horns, three trombones, baritone, and tuba to perform this literature. For other brass choir works see especially the catalogs of Mercury, Associated Music Publishers, Brodt, and Summy-Birchard.)

Bach	Contrapunctus No. 1, No. 3, and No. 5 from Art of Fugue
Beethoven	Three Equale
Brahms	Es ist ein Ros' Entsprungen
Buonamente	Sonata from Sonate et Canzoni (1636)
Buxtehude	Fanfare and Chorus from Ihr lieben Christen
Corelli	Pastorale from Christmas Concerto
Couperin, F.	Fugue on the Kyrie

67

Ehmann	Bläser-Intraden zum Wochenlied (65 chorales of the church year)
Gabrieli, G.	Canzona No. 1, No. 2, No. 3, No. 4
Glazounov	In Modo Religioso, Op. 38
King, R.	Prelude and Fugue
Palestrina	Three Hymns
Pezel	Sonata No. 1, No. 2, No. 3, No. 22, No. 25
Purcell	Music for Queen Mary II
Purcell	Voluntary on Old 100th
	Sonata No. 1, No. 7, No. 18, No. 19, No. 24
Scheidt	Three Christmas Chorales from Tabulaturbuch (1650)
Traditional	Two Medieval Motets
	Christmas Music for Brass (Ed. M. Rasmussen)
	Reformation Chorales

Brass Choir Music with Organ

Bingham	Concerto for Brass and Organ	H. W. Gray
Burnham, Cardon	Festival Chorale	Robert King
Clarke, Jeremiah	Purcell's Trumpet Voluntary	Editions Musicus
Gabrieli	Canzon Duodecimi Toni	Robert King
Schaffer, Robert	Paschal Triptych	Robert King
Sowerby	Festival Musick for Organ, Brass and Kettledrums	H. W. Gray
Widor	O Lord, Save Thy People (Organ, brass, and snare drum)	Mercury

Brass with Voices

Precedents for the composition of large double choir works were set by Giovanni Gabrieli. *In Ecclesiis* calls for one group of two trombones and a violin, another of 3 cornetti, and two four-part choruses. Heinrich Schütz (1585-1672) journeyed from Germany to Italy to study with Gabrieli. From Gabrieli he learned the method of using several choir groups for one composition. A wedding anthem—*Freue dich des Weibes deiner Jugend*—uses two cornetts and three trombones with mixed chorus. The instrumental parts are independent rather than following vocal parts, and there is a seven-measure sinfonia for the instruments alone. Another composition which follows the style initiated by Gabrieli is Benevoli's Mass for the dedication of the Salzburg Cathedral in 1628. It calls for two organs each with an eight-part mixed voice choir, two groups of six string instruments, a woodwind quartet, an ensemble of two cornetti and three trombones and two quartets of trumpets each with timpani. There are also two parts for high trumpets (clarini). Dietrich Buxtehude (ca. 1637-1707) conceived broad effects by dividing instruments into two groups for antiphonal use in the same movement. His wind instrument writing is mostly for cornetti, trombones, trumpets, and bassoons.

Bach's predecessors as church musicians in Leipzig composed various works for voices and brasses. Johann Schein, Tobias Michael, Sebastian Knupfer, Johann Schelle, and Johann Kuhnau, who was Bach's immediate predecessor, all wrote parts for brass instruments in many of their choral compositions. An exceptional Bach cantata, *O Jesus Christ, meins Leben Licht*, is for four voices with winds. A current transcription has parts for four trumpets, two trombones, and mixed voice choir.

Henry Purcell's anthem *Thou Knowest Lord the*

Secrets of Our Hearts, written for the funeral of Queen Mary II, is accompanied by brass quartet doubling the voice parts. The brass played a short march—a dirge—before the anthem and a beautiful canzona following.

Listed here are transcriptions of older cathedral works and some very fine contemporary compositions. It would be advisable before planning performance of brass-with-voices selections to develop a brass ensemble through the use of literature from the preceding section for brass alone. It is not possible to perform this literature without players fully developed both technically and musically.

A few technical hints might be welcomed at this point. The brass player's embouchre is best developed through regular practice of long tones and lip slurs. Even for a church group composed of members already trained elsewhere it is well to commence rehearsals with gradual warm-up procedures such as chords for listening to intonation, tonguing patterns, and short chorales or hymn tunes.

Music for Brass with Voices

SATB: 3 trumpets, trombone or timpani	Bach	Jesu, nun sei gepreiset (German and English)	Robert King
SATB-SATB: 3 trumpets, 2 trombone, tuba, timpani	Beach, P. W.	Rejoice in the Lord	Summy-Birchard
SSATB: 2 trumpets, 2 horns, trombone or; 3 trumpets, 2 trombones	Bender, J.	Psalm 150	Concordia
SATB: 3 trumpets, trombone, organ	Blanchard, W.	An Anthem of Praise	Boston

SSAATB or SSA: 3 trumpets, horn, 2 trombones, baritone, tuba	Brown, Leon	To God Be the Glory	New Choral
SATBB: 4 trumpets, 2 horns, trombones, baritone/ trombone, (tuba), or 3 trumpets and organ	Buxtehude	Fanfare and Chorus (Ihr lieben Christen) (German and English)	Robert King
SSAATTBB: 3 trumpets, timpani, percussion, piano or organ	Daniels	A Psalm of Praise	H. W. Gray
SSA-SATB: 3 trumpets, 1 trumpet, horn, trombone, baritone, tuba	De Lassus	Providebam Dominum	Robert King
SATB: 2 trumpets, trombone, baritone, trombone	Des Prez	Absalom, Fili Mi	Robert King
SSATBB: 3 trumpets, 3 trombones	Dressler	A Trumpet Gloria	J. Fischer
TTBB: 3 horns, 3 trombones, baritone, tuba	Frackenpohl	Shepherds, Rejoice	Robert King
SSAATTBB: 4 trumpets, 4 trombones, organ (tuba)	Gabrieli, G.	Jubilate Deo	G. Schirmer
SATB: 3 trumpets	Hannahs	Hosanna to the Son of David (Palm Sunday)	H. W. Gray
SAB: 2 trumpets, trombone	Hastings (Arr. J. Riedel)	Our Lord Is Risen	Augsburg
SSAATTBB: 3 trumpets, 3 trombones, tuba, percussion, organ	Jolley	Gloria in Excelsis	Shawnee
SSATBB: 2 trumpets, 2 trombones, tuba, percussion	Kirk	O Come, Let Us Sing	Summy-Birchard
SATB: 2 trumpets, 2 trombones	Neff, J.	Four Traditional Carols	Summy-Birchard
SATB or TTBB: 3 trumpets, 3 trombones, tuba	Nelson, R.	Choral Fanfare for Christmas	Boosey & Hawkes
SATB: 2 trumpets, horn, trombone	Nicolai, P.	How Brightly Shines the Morning Star	C. Fischer

71

SATB: 2 trumpets, 2 trombones	Pachelbel (Ed. A. Lovelace)	All Praise and Thanks to God	Brodt
SATB: 3 trumpets, 3 trombones	Pfautsch	Christian! Dost Thou See Them?	Abingdon
SATB: 3 trumpets, 3 trombones, tuba	————	I'll Praise my Maker	Abingdon
SATB: 2 trumpets, 2 trombones	Praetorius	In Dulci Jubilo (German and English)	Robert King
SATB-SATB: 3 trumpets, trombone, and 2 trumpets, trombone, b-flat trombone, or tuba, organ	Schütz	Psalm 150 (German and English)	Robert King
2-part chorus: 2 trumpets, horn, trombone, baritone, tuba, organ	Schütz	See the Fig Tree	Lawson-Gould
SAB: 3 trumpets, timpani, organ	Shrubsole (Arr. W. Rieger)	All Hail the Power of Jesus' Name	Flammer
SATB: soprano solo, 2 trumpets, 2 trombones	Titcomb	Rejoice We All and Praise the Lord	H. W. Gray
SATB: 2 trumpets, 2 trombones	Walton	Fanfare for Easter	Neil A. Kjos
SATB: 3 trumpets, 2 horns, 2 trombones b-flat trombone, baritone, tuba	Ward, W. R.	Father, We Praise Thee	Edward B. Marks
SATB: soprano or tenor solo, 3 trumpets, trombone, organ	Warner, R.	Come, Thou Long Expected Jesus	H. W. Gray

Orchestra

Use of orchestral ensembles in churches has been a gradual development with occasional setbacks. From the beginning of the seventeenth century there are numerous reports of choral performances accompanied by various combinations of instruments. Interesting particulars of the use of instruments in some church pieces by Claudio Monteverdi (1567-1643), grouped together under the title *Sanctissimae Virgini* and printed in 1610, are quoted by Adam Carse in *The History of Orchestration:*

Two cornetti and two violins in turn rush about in thirds or in rapid imitative phrases above a slow-moving bass and vocal parts. . . . Later on in the same work "*Piffari*" ("pipes"=shawms, oboes, or flutes.), violins, cornetti, trombones, and flutes play in succession above a steady bass part, and provide plenty of varied tone-colour. More logical and artistic is the successive use of the well-balanced and contrasted groups: first a group of two violins, tenors and basses, then two cornetti and a trombone, which eventually unite with the choral voices in building up a rich and sonorous ensemble. In another piece two cornetti and three trombones alternate with a body of string instruments, almost the identical instruments used in groups of mixed tone-colour by Gabrieli just about the same time.[2]

Using the usual foundations of strings but adding various woodwind and brass instruments and actually using them for variety or color effects rather than just doubling vocal parts was well established by both Alessandro Stradella (1642-82), and Alessandro Scarlatti (1660-1725). Stradella, in his oratorio *John the Baptist* (about 1676), used this type of orchestra. Scarlatti used for the accompaniment of his oratorios an orchestra consisting of first and second violins, violas,

[2] New York: E. P. Dutton & Company, 1925, p. 46. Used by permission of E. P. Dutton & Company and Routledge Kegan Paul, Ltd.

violoncellos, basses, two oboes, two bassoons, and two horns. Haydn and Mozart also used this instrumentation for many of their works for the church, although sometimes two flutes, two clarinets, and two trumpets were added. In oratorios of the time some composers added timpani and trombones.

Maurizio Cazzati, director of the San Petronio (Bologna) orchestra, was a leader in the seventeenth century composition of orchestral works using one or more trumpets. There were other trumpet sonatas by members of this same orchestra. Albergati, Aldrovandini, Colonna, Franceschini, Perti, Torelli, D. Gabrieli, and G. Jacchini are named by various sources. Researchers report that in the archives of the San Petronio Chapel there are multiple parts for these sonatas indicating they were performed orchestrally rather than as chamber music with one performer on a part.

Following the Italian styles Johann Heinrich Schmelzer (1623-80) in 1662 in Nurnberg in his *Sacro-profanus concentus musicus* scored church selections for violins, violas da gamba, cornettini, trumpets, and trombones. In Salzburg in 1676 Heinrich Biber (1644-1704) wrote his *Sonatae tam aris quam aulis servientes* (appropriate for altar or court) with parts for two trumpets, two violins, two violas, and organ.

Giovanni Gabrieli used an orchestra of eleven violins, eight violas, two violoncelli, three string basses, two cornetti, one bassoon, three trombones, and four theorboe (bass lutes).

Orchestra with Voices

In earlier days the organ, not being as fully developed, frequently was given a less prominent place than it now occupies. It was quite natural to find the organ serving as just the harmonic basis of vocal or instrumental music. The use of instruments other than the organ to assist choral groups reached a high development by Bach, in addition to the fact that he also achieved the most remarkable results as a composer for the organ. The accompaniment for church services always included orchestral instruments. Some of these players were professional musicians; some were students or amateurs. Bach found it necessary to go through channels to request instruments and players. Speaking of the church music at Leipzig in a request to the town council—his employer—he said:

> The number of persons engaged for the church music [instrumental] is 8, namely, 4 Town Pipers (*Stadt Pfeifer*), 3 professional fiddlers (*Kunts Geiger*), and one apprentice. Modesty forbids me to speak at all truthfully of their qualities and musical knowledge. Nevertheless it must be remembered that they are partly *emeriti* and partly not at all in such *exercitio* as they should be.[3]

In his *Short but most necessary draft for a well-appointed Church Music; with certain modest reflections on the decline of the same (1730)*, he desired each church to have an orchestra of two or three first violins,

[3] Hans T. David and Arthur Mendel, *The Bach Reader* (New York: W. W. Norton & Company, 1945), p. 121.

two or three second violins, two first violas, two second violas, two cellos, one bass viol, two or three oboes, one or two bassoons, three trumpets, kettledrums—"eighteen persons at least." [4]

A major portion of Bach's duties as a minister of music in the church was to provide each week a cantata for the Sunday-morning service. Each cantata was composed to be appropriate for the particular season of the church year. The main hymn for the day was the chorale which was used in the cantata and which Bach used as a basis for his organ playing. It was customary for the congregation to sing the closing chorale. Fifty-four of the cantatas end in a chorale with the voices of the choir being doubled by orchestral instruments. In these cantatas the first and last stanzas of the chorale hymn are set in their original text; the others may be freely paraphrased. In each instance the chorale melody is used elaborately for the opening chorus, then in the last movement the chorale appears in typical four-part harmony. These cantatas are not choral works with orchestral accompaniment. The voices and the instruments are of equal significance. Performances which Bach himself conducted frequently had more instrumentalists than singers. The string instruments in those days did not produce as brilliant a tone as those of today, however. Study of the cantatas shows how the use of certain groups of instruments is recurrent in depicting sorrow, joy, con-

[4] *Ibid.*

templation, or exaltation. Although many of the instruments are now obsolete, the music is still effective played with modern instrumentation. European manufacturers are now making available copies of obsolete instruments for those who wish to use the original instrumentation. One of the important facts for church-minded instrumentalists is that many fine compositions for various instrumental ensembles have been arranged based on chorales from the cantatas. Bach treats the chorales in various ways in the cantatas. There are at least four types in particular which instrumentalists should study for better understanding of the arrangements which are likely to be presented to them for concert performance.

1. The simple chorale, a four-part harmonization suitable for congregational singing.

2. The extended chorale, the melody still in four-part harmonization for the voices but the lines may be separated by short orchestral interludes.

3. The embellished or decorated chorale, in which some of the instruments have independent parts.

4. The chorale fantasia, evolved from the organ choral prelude, using all the instruments used in the cantata.

These chorales as harmonized by Bach—and many other chorales from various sources—are characterized by straightforward dignity and the particular beauty exemplified by purity and simplicity.

In France Jean François Le Sueur (1760-1837), who became *maitre de chapelle* of Notre Dame in 1786, engaged a full orchestra and performed many masses and motets. Although popular he retired in 1788 because of various oppositions. His music includes ten oratorios, over thirty masses, a Stabat Mater, Psalms, and Motets. Hector Berlioz (1803-69) was one of his pupils. When Berlioz' *Requiem Mass* was performed for the first time (1837) in Notre Dame Cathedral an orchestra of 130 instruments, including 16 kettle-drums, was used, and in addition in the *Tuba Mirum* there are four separate groups of brass instruments typifying the trumpets calling from the four corners of the earth on the day of the Last Judgment. By this time many cathedral and other church orchestras were permanently endowed. In Germany some of these survived to modern times in Dresden, Breslau, Munich, and Vienna.

In the eighteenth century while the oratorio was popular in England Handel was using orchestral accompaniments and wrote concertos to be used as interludes in his oratorios. These were considered an added attraction for the audience. He wrote a series of sixteen concertos for organ and small orchestra. Handel's *Chandos Anthems*, written during 1718-20 for services at the chapel of the Duke of Chandos, near London, expanded the form of the anthem toward the dimensions of a cantata. Organ and strings were used, with one oboe, one bassoon, and sometimes two flutes. Henry Purcell wrote numerous anthems with strings. Some of these have interludes for strings alone.

Sometime between 1767 and 1780 Mozart wrote

seventeen *Epistle Sonatas* for use in the Cathedral of
Salzburg where he was organist. They are for organ
and strings except that in Nos. 12 and 14 oboes, trumpets, and timpani are added. These sonatas were played
between the Epistle and the Gospel. They radiate pleasant cheerfulness, beauty of form, uncomplicated harmonization, and charming orchestration. They are not
ecclesiastically solemn. Mozart's faith in the divinity
was certainly not doleful.

Many times festival anthems, cantatas, and oratorios
are performed with a substituted keyboard accompaniment instead of the orchestral parts which the composer prepared. This results in a production quite different from the composer's intention. The orchestras
of Bach, Handel, and Purcell were certainly important, in most instances vital, to the performance of
their works. Even though modern substitutions must
sometimes be made, an orchestral group is preferable
to a keyboard reduction.

Newspaper accounts of sacred concerts presented in
New York, Boston, Philadelphia, and Charleston,
South Carolina, between 1730 and 1800 demonstrate
the popularity of orchestral ensembles—and also instrumental solos—particularly for the production of
oratorio style concerts. The typical concert of those
days consisted of vocal solos, chiefly from the works of
Handel, interspersed with one or two anthems or
choruses and one or two instrumental solos, commencing with an orchestral overture and closing with an
orchestral finale. A few of these concerts were held in

theaters but most were held in churches. Frequently mentioned as the opening selection was Martini's *Celebrated Overture*. The *Grand Symphony* of Pleyel was performed at a concert at St. Peter's Church in Salem, Massachusetts, on November 25, 1790. The purpose of the concert was to raise money to repair the organ!

On April 8, 1796, the *Charleston City Gazette* listed the instrumentation of the orchestra that would assist the performance of the "celebrated Stabat Mater of Doctor Haydn": "one organ, 12 violins, 3 basses, 5 tenors, 6 oboes, flutes and clarinets, two horns, one bassoon and two pair of kettle drums, in all 30." Apparently several musicians played more than one instrument.

Although the Collegium Musicum of the Bethlehem Settlement (Pennsylvania) of the Moravians is one of the earliest American orchestras of which there is definite record, even earlier than the Moravians there had been other Pennsylvanians laying the foundations for church music that included instruments. One of the fascinating personalities of the German Pietists was Johannes Kelpius. Kelpius was twenty-one when with, about forty others, he arrived in America in 1694. He and his followers went to Germantown, acquired land on the Wissahickon, a tributary of Schulkill River— now a creek in Fairmount Park in Philadelphia—and constructed a forty-feet square tabernacle for religious and musical services and their housing. Called Hermits of the Ridge, or Mystics of the Wissahickon, they referred to themselves as "The Contented of the God-loving Soul." In the tabernacle there was choral and instrumental music using some type of organ and instruments such as viols, oboes, trumpets, and kettledrums. Kelpius and his colleagues furnished instrumental music for the consecration of the Swedish Lutheran (Gloria Dei) Church at Wicaco (Philadelphia), July 2, 1700. One of Kelpius' group, Justus Falckner, was ordained in this same church November 24, 1703. For the ordination service the Mystics of the Wissahickon again furnished the music. The service was opened with a voluntary "on the little organ in the gallery, by Jonas, the organist," and supplemented by "the viol, hautboy, trumpets, and kettledrums." [5]

The Bethlehem Settlement of the Moravians started in 1742, and records refer to many song services accompanied by violins, flutes, and horns. String and wind instruments are frequently mentioned as adding to the solemnity of worship, and there is also much mention of their uses in the recreation of the various groups. The Reverend Immanuel Nitschman, a violinist, became the leader of the Moravian orchestra known as the Collegium Musicum in 1761. The Bethlehem musicians were also composers. Between 1745 and 1840 they wrote many original compositions. Of particular interest are copies of six trios for strings and of the symphonies which are preserved in the archives of the Moravian church. Although instruments and music were imported from Europe, much music was

[5] From the *Diary of Kelpius* with annotations by J. F. Sachse, Pennsylvania German Society Proceedings (1913-14), Vols. 24-25.

copied and many instruments were made in the settlement. Historians report that nowhere in the country could one hear anthems with instrumental accompaniment on the scale used in the Moravian communities. This story is told about the use of instruments in church services: When a zealous young minister questioned the propriety of using the same instruments in church on Sunday which had been used for secular music the evening before, one of his elders asked, "Will you use the same mouth to preach with to day which you now use in eating sausage?" [6]

There are Moravian music manuscripts dated 1761 by Jeremiah Dencke. To him is given credit for introducing solo and chorus anthems into the church service. Some of his scores call for strings, flutes, and horns.

American church orchestras today may be composed of elementary school children from the church school, junior-high and high-school youth, mixed groups of amateurs, or professional musicians. Several major symphonies have performed in such churches as Riverside Church, New York City; Rockefeller Memorial Church, Chicago; and National Presbyterian Church, Washington, D. C. First Methodist Church in Evanston, Illinois, presented the Northwestern University Orchestra conducted by Dr. Thor Johnson during the Handel Festival in 1959. These are but a few examples

[6] Rufus A. Grider, *Historical Notes on Music in Bethlehem, Pennsylvania, from 1741 to 1871* (Philadelphia: Printed for J. Hill Martin, by John L. Pile, 1873).

of the larger groups. Numerous performances are now being made by smaller orchestras.

The need today is care in the choice of literature and attention to those details which result in a churchly performance. Persons who play in church orchestras, whether amateur or professional, must be helped to understand that their function is essentially one of refreshment of the human spirit with an attitude of humble joy attained by corporate worship.

Orchestra Music

Selected List for String Orchestra

Bach	Fugue—The Great (G minor)	M P H
————	Jesu, Joy of Man's Desiring	Oxford
————	Mystical Adoration	Volkwein
————	Our Father in Heaven	Associated Music Publishers
Bach (Watson)	We All Believe in One God	Witmark
Brahms	Es ist ein Ros' entsprungen	Oxford
Bush, C.	Natus Est Immanuel	Galaxy
Byrd	An Earthly Tree, a Heavenly Fruit	Galaxy
Corelli	Concerto Grosso, Op. 6, No. 8	Associated Music Publishers
————	Sonata da Chiesa in E Minor, Op. 1.	Associated Music Publishers
Creston	Gregorian Chant	Shawnee
Gaul, H.	Suite Ecclesiasticus	J. Fischer
Healey, W.	Chorale Prelude: Puer nobis nascitur	Condoria
Howard, J.	Still Waters: Reverie on a Psalm Tune	Editions Musicus
Manfredini, F.	Christmas Concerto	Associated Music Publishers

83

| Tartini | Sinfonia Pastorale in D | Associated Music Publishers |
| Vaughan Williams | Fantasia on a Theme by Thomas Tallis (Double string orchestra) | G. Schirmer |

Music for string orchestra and organ

Bach	Sinfonias from the Cantatas (3)	Associated Music Publishers
Corelli	Eight Concerti da Chiesa, Op. 6	Peters
Handel	Twelve Concerti Grossi, Op. 6	Peters
La Tombelle	I Am the Resurrection and the Life (Organ, strings, and two oboes)	Baron
Torelli	Christmas Concerto, Op. 8, No. 6	Associated Music Publishers
Valentini, G.	Christmas Pastorale	Associated Music Publishers

Music for small orchestra (strings and listed winds)

Bach, C. P. E.	Sinfonia in F Major (2 flutes, 2 oboes, 2 horns, bassoon)	Peters
Bach	Jesus suffered Pain and Death (solo flute)	Volkwein
———	Sheep May Safely Graze (flute, clarinet)	Volkwein
Bach (Exposito)	Sleepers, Wake! (flute, oboe, clarinet, trumpet, bassoon, trombone, horn)	Oxford
Darke	Meditation on Brother James' Air (solo flute)	Oxford
Dittersdorf	Overture to Esther (2 oboes, 2 bassoons, 2 horns)	Krebs

84

Grabner	Abendmusik, Op. 25 (flute, oboe, clarinet, horn, bassoon)	Kahnt
Handel (Holst)	Pastoral Symphony (flute, clarinet)	Volkwein
Heinichen	Pastorale per la della notte nativitate Christi (2 oboes, 2 flutes)	Boosey & Hawks
McCollins	All Glory Laud and Honor (2 horns, trumpet, trombone)	Ricordi

Music for Full Orchestra

Bach (Cailliet)	Fervent Is My Longing	Elkan Vogel
Bach (Cailliet)	Little Fugue in G Minor	C. Fischer
Bach (Marcelli)	All Glory Be to God on High	C. Fischer
Bach (Stokowski)	Chorale from Easter Cantata	Broude
Bach (Stokowski)	Adagio from Toccata and Fugue in C	Broude
Bach (Tolmage)	Now Let Every Tongue Adore Thee	Staff
Brahms	O God, Thou Holiest (Chorale Prelude)	Broude
Kindler	Three Seventeenth Century Dutch Tunes (In times of stress, See how strong, Wilt now walk before the Lord)	C. Fischer
Luther (Gardner)	A Mighty Fortress Is Our God	Staff
Palestrina (Harvey)	Adoramus te and Sanctus	Elkan Vogel
Spelman	Christ and the Blind Man (Symphonic poem for orchestra and piano)	H. W. Gray

85

| Yon | Concerto Gregoriano | J. Fischer |
| | (Organ and orchestra) | |

Music for choir and orchestra (SATB with orchestra unless otherwise noted)

Antes Ed. Johnson and McCorkle	Shout Ye Heavens (SATB with organ and/or 2 horns or trumpets and strings)	Boosey & Hawkes
Bach	Jesu, Joy of Man's Desiring	Oxford
————	Lord, Christ, We Now Thy Praises Sing	Oxford
————	A Mighty Fortress Is Our God	Witmark
Bach (Ehret)	Sanctus	Boosey & Hawkes
Crüger (Cailliet)	Now Thank We All Our God	Boosey & Hawkes
Gounod	Unfold Ye Portals	C. Fischer
Haydn	The Heavens Are Telling	C. Fischer
Mozart	Exsultate, Jubilate (Motet for Soprano and orchestra)	Associated Music Publishers
Shaw	Rocking O Little One Garden of Jesus The Cradle (The four for Unison or SATB with strings)	Oxford
Teschner (Cain)	Glory, Laud and Honor	Flammer
Vaughan Williams	Fantasia on Christmas Carols	Galaxy
————	The Hundredth Psalm	Galaxy

Cantatas with Orchestral Parts

| Whear | Forever Thy Word, Alleluia | Ludwig |
| Avshalomov | How Long, Oh Lord
(Mixed chorus, contralto
solo, and orchestra) | Edwards B. Marks |

Bach	Psalm CXXI (SATB with organ and orchestra)	C. Fischer
Bunjes	Comfort Ye My People (Extended Chorale (Cantata) for mixed chorus, strings, and organ	Concordia
Buxtehude	Every Word and Thought (SATB, Violin I, II, Viola I, II, Cello, Bass, and organ)	Concordia
Mendelssohn	Come Unto Him (SATB and solos with strings)	C. Fischer
Schütz Ed. Gore	The Seven Words of Jesus Christ on the Cross (SSATB, five soloists, strings, and organ)	Concordia

Other Large Choral Works with Orchestra

Bach	The St. Luke Passion (Strings and two oboes)	C. Fischer
Daniels, M.	Exultate Deo	Summy-Birchard
Dello Joio	A Psalm of David (SATB with brass, strings, and percussion or piano)	C. Fischer
Holst, G.	The Coming of Christ (Full chorus, incidental soprano and alto solos, trumpet, organ, and piano)	G. Schirmer
Lalande	Dixit Dominus (Psalm 109) (Soloists, chorus, and orchestra)	Mercury
Montgomery, B.	Oxford Requiem	Novello-Gray
Pergolesi	Stabat Mater (Strings, organ, SA solos, SA chorus)	Associated Music Publishers
Rogers, B.	The Exodus, Sacred Poem	Summy-Birchard

87

——————— (Solo voices, chorus, and
                    orchestra)
——————— The Raising of Lazarus   Summy-Birchard
                    (Solo voices, chorus, and
                    orchestra)

NOTE: Oxford University Press and G. Schirmer both have many
      works for mixed chorus and orchestra with the orchestral
      parts available on rental.

Wind Ensemble and Concert Band

Many members of youth fellowship groups and church-school classes are also members of the local school band. Both the director of music and the band director are concerned with the musical development of these persons, as well as with the performance of religious music. Rather than compete against each other for prestige or for students' time, these two community leaders should combine their efforts for mutual benefit to school and church. Frequently the school band director is a part time church organist or choir director. Whether the leadership is shared by one or two persons, it is easy to co-ordinate religious and music education functions.

The school band is invited to play for various community events. Frequently the occasion calls for serious music. It may be a Memorial Day service in the cemetery, an Easter sunrise service, a Thanksgiving service, or a festival service sponsored by united churches. The band may need religious music for school programs, commencement, or baccalaureate. Such occasions enable the group to demonstrate its ability not only to march and entertain, but also to present serious music played in a manner conducive to worship.

A church musician looking for an opportunity to co-ordinate school and church effort may suggest to the local organization of ministers that the band director be invited to present a program of wind ensemble music in the church for a Sunday afternoon or evening Vesper service. This occasion provides a good opportunity to combine band and chorus if desired. Each group might present several numbers alone, joining for a thrilling climax. The best band music for such an occasion is that which reflects joyous dignity. It should not be flippant or frivolous, nor should it sound funereal. Good music requires a certain amount of concentration or contemplation. The best band music is comparable to churchly organ music, remaining dignified without overdramatic effects. Fortunately there is an increasing amount of appropriate music available at all levels of difficulty.

Preparation for a program of this nature directs attention to acoustics, particularly if the church is small or does not have a high ceiling. A few experiments in rehearsals will indicate which seating arrangement is best. If the band is too large, it may be necessary to select a small ensemble for a program. If the church has a balcony experiment with antiphonal groups. When rehearsing sacred music for a church service band members will listen more attentively and become conscious of the need to improve tone qualities. When preparing for this type program make certain that all participants fully understand the nature of the event, the procedures to be employed, and details of the prescribed wearing apparel. Be sure publicity for the program is absolutely accurate. Public performance of religious music gives the band, its director, and the listeners a very satisfying experience in aesthetic growth.

By co-ordinating his efforts with those of the school band director the church musician increases his sphere of influence. The band director may ask him for assistance in choosing appropriate music for community events, and a spirit of co-operation will be engendered. The Church today should not remain isolated from other institutions, and the church musician can strengthen the outreach of his church in the community.

Musical Resources for Bands

Grade I—Elementary (easy)

Bach (Gordon)	Grand Finale from Cantata No. 207	Bourne
Bach (Petersen)	Air from Suite No. 3 in D	Henri Elkan
Bach (Mairs)	Christ Lay in Bonds of Death	Bourne
Carter	Motet for Band	Charles H. Hansen
Croft-Koehler (Ormsby)	O God, Our Help in Ages Past	Bourne
Gordon	Three Hymns by Palestrina	Bourne
Haydn-Brahms (Tolmage)	Chorale: St. Antoni	Staff
Leisring (Houseknecht)	God of All Nations	Neil Kjos
Lockhart	Graded Chorales for Band	Music Publishers

Luther (Gardner)	A Mighty Fortress Is Our God	Staff
Marcello (Whitney)	Psalm 18	Bourne
Mozart (Tolmage)	Hymn of Praise (Ave Verum)	Staff
Petersen	Grant Unto Us Peace	Kendor
Rachmaninoff (Houseknecht)	Glory and Honor	Neil Kjos
Tschesnekoff-Wagner (Houseknecht)	Salvation Is Created and Awake	Neil Kjos
Wagner-Brahms-Franck (Arr. Gordon)	Three Modern Chorales	Bourne
Wienhorst	Choice Chorales and Hymns for Band	Concordia

Grade II—Intermediate (medium)

Bach (Leidzen)	Jesu, Joy of Man's Desiring	C. Fischer
Bach (Leidzen)	Komm, süsser Tod (Come, Sweet Death)	C. Fischer
Bach (Moehlmann)	Prelude and Fugue in B Flat Major	Music Publishers
Bach (Whitney)	In Thee Is Gladness	Bourne
Bruckner (Schoettle)	Gloria from Mass No. 2 in E Minor	Edward B. Marks
Franck (Wilson)	Panis Angelicus	C. Fischer
Guilmant (Righter)	Choral March and Fugue	C. Fischer
Handel (Mairs)	Prelude and Fugue in D Minor	Edward B. Marks
Leidzen	Chorale Prelude on the Doxology	Leeds
————	Chorale Prelude on Lead, Kindly Light	Chappell

Palestrina (Harvey)	Adoremus Te and Sanctus	Elkan-Vogel
Pierne-Cheyette	In the Cathedral	G. Schirmer
Reed-Houseknecht	Slavonic Folk Suite	Charles H. Hansen
Strauss	Allerseelen	Ludwig
Williams	Testament of Nations	Schmitt, Hall & McCreary

Grade III—Advanced (moderately difficult)

Bach (Frackenpohl)	Five Chorales	Shawnee
Bach (Leidzen)	Arioso	C. Fischer
Bach (Malin)	From Heaven Above	Neil Kjos
Bach (Schoettle)	Prelude in C Minor	Edward B. Marks
Hanson	Chorale and Alleluia	C. Fischer
Jacob	Fantasia on the Alleluia Hymn	Chappell
Leidzen	Hymn of Thanksgiving	Leeds
————	Holy, Holy, Holy	Bourne
Luther (Bach-Lillya)	A Mighty Fortress Is Our God	C. Fischer

Grade IV—Advanced (difficult)

Bach (Leidzen)	Toccata and Fugue in D Minor	C. Fischer
Work	Portraits from the Bible 1. Moses 2. Ruth 3. Shadrach, Meschach, Abednego	Shawnee

Mixed Chorus with Band Accompaniment

Gillett-Dahnert	Come, Christians, Join to Sing Alleluia!	Summy-Birchard
Kempinski-Bristol	Gracious Lord Who Givest Blessing	Leeds
Latham	Psalm 130	Summy-Birchard

INDEX